2-16-76   aw-1.98

THE
HELLFIRE
COOKBOOK

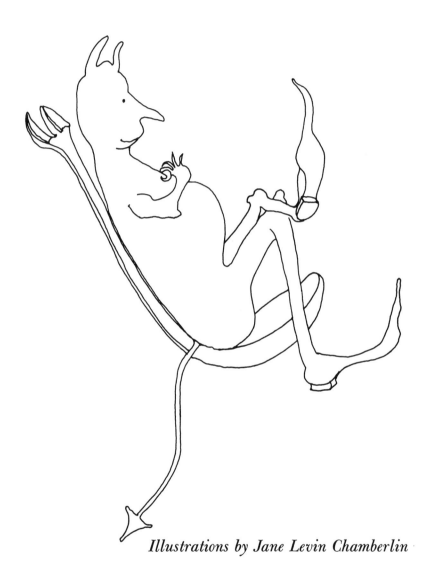

Illustrations by Jane Levin Chamberlin

THE HELLFIRE COOKBOOK

Recipes For Fiery Food For Those Who Like It,

And For Those Others Who,

Because Of The Sin Of Gluttony,

Should Become Used To It Here And Now

Ere They Perforce Eat It Hereafter

When They Will Need A Long Spoon.

John Philips Cranwell

QUADRANGLE

The New York Times Book Co.

Library of Congress Cataloging in Publication Data

Cranwell, John Philips, 1904–
    The hellfire cookbook.

    Includes index.
    1. Cookery, International. 2. Spices. I. Title.
TX725.A1C64   1975   641.6′3′84   74-24278
ISBN 0-8129-0528-8

Book design: Tere LoPrete

For Rosemary

Without whose expert bibliographic midwifery, experimental cooking, tasting, typing, infernal suggestions, and perpetual nagging this book would still be half in my kitchen and half in my typewriter.

Contents

Preface

PLEASE read this Preface. The plea is made for your own benefit. Be he chef, historian, economist, or philosopher, the writer usually includes in this part of his work his purpose and what the reader should expect to find. If you skip the Preface in haste to reach the meat of the matter you may lose some of the seasoning.

Rarely can the exact place, date, and hour of a conception be pinpointed. I conceived this book at the Fujiya Hotel in the Hakone National Park of Japan at four o'clock in the morning. I know the exact hour because I looked at my watch. I woke up with the idea taking shape in my mental womb. Almost everyone at one time or another wakes up in the mid-portion of the night and conceives brilliant ideas. Unfortunately, in the bright light of day the conceptions abort. They are mostly impractical, and sometimes downright silly. In this case, however, the conception seemed even more brilliant at high noon and over the first martini than it had eight hours earlier. Even the name of the brainchild had taken a turn for the better.

The more I considered the conception of a hellfire cookbook, the more I thought, and still think, that every cookbook shelf should hold a volume containing recipes exclusively for fiery food. Please note that I use the word *fiery* throughout to distinguish between dishes which are made hot by seasonings as opposed to dishes made hot in an oven or over a flame.

Any dish can be made fiery by adding cayenne or other peppers, or by using curry powder. What I present is a representative selection of dishes, from canapés to salads, which from their inception were intended to be fiery and not so made by condiments not included in the original recipes.

Fond as I am of fiery food, I would not suggest that you compile an entire menu from these recipes. But many people now and again enjoy a fiery dish as part of a meal. No single book could include all fiery food. Here are enough different kinds of such dishes to enable you to use one or another for any given part of any given meal. *The Hellfire Cookbook* is a selection, not a compendium.

To some extent I have been motivated by philosophical and theological considerations. Gluttony is one of the seven deadly sins punished in Hell by serving the culprit the most fiery of foods. For those who practice gluttony this book should, if properly used, provide gradual immunization to such food hereafter. I do not expect, but do deserve, gratitude for this eleemosynary effort on behalf of my fellows. It is that kind of charity which should and does begin at home.

Two types of food, salads and desserts, were troublesome. Both are usually bland. The second problem was easily resolved. No one who writes a hellfire cookbook can do so without learning the geography of Hell from Dante. In *The Inferno* he points out that in the lowest circle of his satanic majesty's realm, the residents are tormented by icy cold. Hence any very cold recipe, paradoxically, could be used in a hellfire cookbook. Then, too, many desserts are flamed. In this instance at least, you could, so to speak, have your cake and eat it too: cold for the ninth circle and flaming for others.

Salads admit to no such simple solution. You might almost say of them: that few are born fiery, none achieve fieriness, and some have fire thrust upon them by highly seasoned dressings. I think the salads will meet the norm I have established. They are fiery.

Lest there be thought that this collection owes aught to either the Hell Fire Club of England, founded by Sir Francis Dashwood at Medmenham, or to the Hell Fire Club of Dublin, I utterly deny any such association, much as I might have enjoyed membership in either. The records, including the menus at Medmenham, were burned by the organization's secretary. All records of the Irish fraternity were burned, when, in the words of the Irish cultural attaché in Washington, the clubhouse near Dublin "appropriately went up in flames." Alas, and I mean alas, I cannot produce a single dish which can be traced definitely to either of those eighteenth-century groups of devil worshippers and hedonists. While their chefs were no doubt expert seasoners, the modern cook should know something about taste sampling for fiery food.

Tasting dishes for fieriness is far different from tasting for salt. A half-teaspoon sampling will tell you immediately whether the dish lacks salt or has too much; if the latter, you have a problem. Such a sampling when testing for fire is no gauge until you have swallowed the sample. If the fire is immediately noticeable, which is unlikely, you have too much. Only after you have waited several moments to allow the backlash to become effective can you judge how fiery in fact the dish is. The fire comes back from the gullet to the tongue. If, after two tastings, you still get no backlash you have a smolder and not a fire.

One additional point: in many instances the "fire" in seasonings does not become apparent until the seasoning has been cooked. Curry provides an excellent example. If you make your own curry powder, the combination before it is cooked will seem bland. If you use commercial curry powder it too will be bland until it has been cooked, usually in some kind of shortening with other seasonings such as chopped onions and garlic. Most fiery dishes should be tasted about halfway through cooking. Then you can determine with accuracy whether they need additional fire. Like salt, fiery seasonings are easy to add and almost impossible to remove.

Finding these recipes, cooking and eating the dishes, and writing this book has been great fun. May you have as much fun using it as I have had in making it.

Acknowledgments

I think it fair to say that this brainchild had two midwives. The first is my wife who bore with me through my bookish pregnancy, corrected my infinite errors in spelling, and tasted dishes she thought repugnant. Hers was that kind of empathy which some men share with their wives during *their* pregnancies: yearnings for unusual food or mad combinations at unreasonable hours, subsequent morning sickness, and the pains of typing labor when you type badly.

The other midwife in this creation was my amanuensis, Rosemary Cartwright to whom I have dedicated the book. She cannot spell either, but her infinite patience with a lazy cook who always looked for shortcuts, her constant good humor, her sailing trips in the Caribbean and across the Atlantic when she left me for weeks at a time to recover her calm, clearly demonstrated her intense efforts to insure the safe delivery of a sound and intelligent brainchild. She, too, tasted, made acrid comments, and frequently provided and tested many of these recipes. I must acknowledge here too, my debt to Francesca Rademaekers who adroitly came to my assistance by filling the gaps created by Rosemary when she was all at sea.

I thank with much pleasure my friend B. Lansdown, to whom I had the honor and privilege of dedicating my last book, for her instructions in many matters pertaining to cookery, especially pastry, and for her amused corrections of my cooking errors.

Then there are the Hutchisons, Greg and Mary. How can I thank them adequately? They contributed recipes, they tasted others, they criticized my cooking and my prose. How can a chef do better when faced by fearful decisions than to have on either hand a Hutchison? The chef may not always like or agree with their decisions, but he knows they are sincere.

I wish to express here, too, my deep gratitude to Hazel Detwiler of Myrtle Hill who owns the only licensed bidet in the Maryland Free State and whose husband, Don, bakes superlative bread. She will attempt anything culinary. Her attempts are uniformly successful. Much have I learned from her, and many goodly dishes have I eaten in her remarkable kitchen.

It would be most ungracious, even snide, to omit mention of my dear, much-traveled friend, and eminent gourmet, Peterkin Pepit who has presented me many a time with unusual recipes collected on his wanderings in strange places. It would be equally ungracious not to mention the research of Mrs. Elizabeth S. Hart which contributed so much to the Introduction.

Finally I wish to thank the publishers of my last book, *A World of Hearty Soups*, Funk & Wagnalls, Co., Inc., for their kind permission to reproduce in this volume the recipes for Philadelphia pepper pot and dahl.

THE
HELLFIRE
COOKBOOK

Introduction

When you acquired this book, no doubt you thought you were getting a collection of recipes for chemically hot or fiery dishes. You were. You were also getting the culinary results of millennia of economic, cultural, maritime, and to a lesser extent, military history.

All fiery food derives its heat from spices, whether they be the chili peppers of Central and South America, the pepper of India, the ginger of Malaysia, or the cloves and other condiments of the Moluccas, also known as the Spice Islands. With the exception of grain, spices and the search for them did more to promote trade, and the so-called Voyages of Discovery, establish cities and colonies, and provoke military action than any other single commodity including gold, gems, and missionary zeal.

When Marco Polo, the renowned Venetian traveler and diplomat for Kublai Khan, returned to Venice in 1295, he brought with him knowledge of the real sources of spices, a secret kept by Arab traders for 3,000 years. Considering the distances involved and the modes of transportation available the return of the Venetian to his home was a feat comparable to Neil Armstrong's return to earth after his visit to the moon. It might well be argued that the latter's journey may have had less significance than the former's. After all, that ancient mariner returned with information vital to world trade and discovery; the spaceman brought back some rocks, and as yet unevaluated information. Polo's memoirs, dictated in 1298 in a Genoese prison, copied and distributed slowly throughout Europe during the fourteenth century, led to the voyages of Columbus, the Cabots, Diaz, Da Gama, Magellan, and Hudson. Their intent in each case was to find a direct route from Europe to the Indies, where Marco Polo said the spices originated, in order to procure and return them to Europe without going through Arabs and other middlemen. Before such a route between the spice-producing countries and Europe was developed by Europeans, the value of cloves, for example, increased ten times between the Moluccas and Malacca;

ginger three times from Calicut to the entrepot at Alexandria; and Indian pepper thirty times between its origin and Venice, a highly important distribution point for the rest of Europe. These enormous increases were caused by the vicissitudes of travel: broken-down camels and bandits by land; shipwreck and pirates by sea. Because of the reduction in the dangers of transportation, Vasco da Gama reported a profit of 400 percent from his first journey to, and spice-laden return from, the Malabar Coast.

The quest for direct sea routes between Europe and the Indies in search of spices had other and more far-reaching results. In 1493, the great Borgia Pope, Alexander VI, in his infallible wisdom divided the unexplored lands into two spheres of influence or conquest. His dividing line ran south through the Atlantic roughly along the 38th meridian. Exploitation of all newly discovered areas east of the line was the prerogative of Portugal; all that to the west, the prerogative of Spain. Later, by treaty between the two countries, the line was shifted to the 45th meridian, thus placing what is now Brazil in the Portuguese sphere.

Meanwhile Columbus had discovered Central America and the islands of the Caribbean. Later, the Portuguese, still searching for spices, scalloped down the West African coast and discovered the Azores, the Cape Verde Islands, Angola, and the Cape of Good Hope, at all of which they established "factories"—later to become colonies—to provide food for revictualing the ships to follow. After rounding the Cape, the Portuguese repeated the process going up the east coast as far as Mombasa, establishing similar factories, especially one in Mozambique.

Eventually it was Da Gama who reached the Malabar Coast of India and in 1512 his compatriots, led by the Portuguese explorer Magellan, found the Moluccas—which included Ternate where the Portuguese set up their headquarters, and Amboina, later a Dutch headquarters.

As a result of the edict of Alexander VI, the Spaniards, taking the Pacific route to the Indies found by Magellan, now in the employ of Charles V of Spain, discovered the Philippines, Indonesia, and other spice-producing islands in the area. Later Charles V sold the Spanish interests in Indonesia to his brother-in-law, John III of Portugal, thus giving the Portuguese, for a time, virtual control of spice-producing areas.

The Portuguese lost no time in consolidating their position and enlarging their potential. They established an enclave at Goa which lasted until the middle of this century. By 1536 they were firmly established and still are at Macao, at the mouth of the Pearl River, thus giving them access to Chinese trade. In 1542, they signed the first commercial treaty with Japan. By then Lisbon had replaced Venice as the European distribution center for spices, and the city on the Tagus outshone the Queen of the Adriatic. The Portuguese had turned dominance of the spice-producing areas into a monopoly of the spice trade, and much other oriental commerce as well.

Most of the Portuguese success was due to their own enterprise and good management, but part of it came from the fact that potential and actual rivals were preoccupied with other, to them, more vital matters than spices. Having found gold, silver, and precious gems in Central and South America and its new colonies in the Pacific, Spain abandoned the pursuit of spices in favor of treasure, colonization, and conversion of the heathen to the true faith. For a time at least Spain seems to have had the better bet.

Spain, too, was engaged in strife north of the Pyrenees, especially in Flanders whose natives, essentially the Dutch, were trying to throw the rascals out. Spain, France, the Papal States, and other Italian city-states—divided into many factions—were all fighting among themselves. Venice, whose commercial star was falling, was trying to maintain its former monopoly of Mediterranean trade against the onslaught of the Genoese. The English, who later played, through the East India Company, so important a part in the spice business, were having their own troubles with France, Scotland, and Spain. The King of Spain was seriously annoyed by the attacks of English seamen and gentlemen-adventurers not only on his colonies in the West Indies and Central America, but also on the Spanish plate ships. Although England disclaimed such attacks, in later years Queen Elizabeth knighted the chief offender, Francis Drake, which did not ease relations between the two countries. In addition, England was torn at this time by political and religious turmoil. Who was to succeed Henry VIII? First it was Mary, the Catholic, then Elizabeth, the Protestant. The infighting was fierce.

In short, the only nations which could have challenged the Portuguese monopoly in spices were so deeply involved with their own or their immediate neighbor's affairs, they had neither the desire nor the ability to disrupt the Portuguese traders.

About a century after the Portuguese had begun to consolidate their empire in the East, the Dutch, with the help of the English, broke the yoke of Spain, and themselves undertook to attack the Portuguese monopoly in the spice business. Except for the English, the Dutch alone had the capability. Italy was still disrupted by internal strife, Spain after Drake's great raid on Cadiz and the resultant destruction of the Armada, was hard put to maintain its American and Pacific colonies, and thought only of protecting its vital treasure galleons beset as they were by Atlantic storms, privateers, and pirates. France seethed with political reform and religious wars; she was engaged, too, in struggles with various continental enemies.

The Dutch, then, were comparatively free to pursue their own path of conquest, opposed only by the Portuguese. Following the latter's routes down the African coast, they established a settlement at Capetown, driving out the Portuguese. Later they took Mauritius off the west coast of India, and while forcing the Portuguese out of their Far East possessions except for Goa and Macao, established two stations in Persia, twelve in India, six in Ceylon, and set up fortified posts throughout the East Indies with headquarters on Amboina. These conquests were the work not of the government but of a private organization, the Dutch East India Company, founded in 1602 by the amalgamation of a number of small Dutch trading groups.

Having driven out the Portuguese, the Dutch for a while enjoyed the former's domination of the spice trade with Europe. They were good but strict colonizers and great seamen. While the company's representatives in the Indies were enjoined to treat the natives fairly, they were also ordered to be firm. They were. Spices were, above all, as valuable then as diamonds later became in the Rand of South Africa. The penalty was death for any unauthorized person to possess or sell a stick of cinnamon. Much later, when representatives of the British East India Company established a post on Amboina, the Dutch quietly went down and massacred the lot. For this deed of violence perpetrated by citizens of a country not at war with the nation of the victims, Oliver Cromwell, then Lord Protector of England, demanded and got from the Dutch government a payment of 390,000 pounds sterling. But Dutch control of spices was not to last so long as that of the people they had displaced. The English under Elizabeth and after the Armada had begun to flex their empire-building muscles. When Drake returned from his circumnavigation of the globe in 1580, he brought many tales of the riches of the

Orient and especially of the spices and silks available there. For almost two decades the English were much too occupied with affairs nearer home to exploit Drake's information. Then, in 1600, Queen Elizabeth chartered the East India Company, which was bent on finding spices and other riches in the Indies. Five years later, the English Moscovy Company employed the English navigator Henry Hudson to find a north*east* passage to the Indies. He failed. The Dutch East India Company commissioned him to find a north*west* passage to the Indies; he found his river. The following year English merchants sent him to find the same passage. He discovered Hudson Bay but no new route to the riches of India. He had contributed, nonetheless, to the founding of other companies and fortunes built on the fur trade of two centuries later. Once again a search for spices resulted in the discovery of new lands and the exploration of a new continent.

Hudson's voyages, however, were not the first efforts by the English to find a passage to India. Five years after Columbus failed to reach the Indies but found a new world, English merchants hired John Cabot and his son Sebastian, Venetians both, to seek a route to the land of spices. John's attempts failed to find a north*west* passage but did find Cape Breton, the west coast of Greenland, Baffin Island, and Newfoundland. Sebastian, after exploring the La Plata for Charles V of Spain, was employed by a group of English merchants to find a north*east* passage to India. The expedition did not achieve its goal but resulted in trade between his employers and the Moscovite merchants.

While shareholders of the East India Company were originally concerned with breaking the Dutch spice-trade monopoly, in which they never quite succeeded—Holland held Indonesia, for example, until the end of World War II—the English company took over the entire subcontinent of India, and policed it with its own army. As a matter of fact, the East India Company became, in the 250 years of its existence, the most powerful private organization in the world. Even the great Hudson's Bay Company which made and un-made fortunes in furs and rum, played a remote second fiddle to the East India Company, whose early voyages resulted in large profits to England. After one voyage, one director stated that the profits from it alone would defray the expense of a navy. And East India seamen, heavily armed and with well-disiplined crews, were seldom prey of enemy privateers or even light ships of war. The company itself made treaties with sovereign princes, it took territories by force of arms, and eventually handed over intact to Britain an enormous well-organized territory with its own civil service, military, and police forces. All started by the quest for spices.

The company's English monopoly of the trade with India and the Spice Islands was abolished in 1833. Twenty years later, after Queen Victoria had bailed out the company following the mutiny, India became the brightest star of the Empire and Victoria became an empress thanks to the shrewd statesmanship of Disraeli. The merchant organization responsible for the conquest of India was dissolved, but once again the desire for spices had resulted in discovery, war, conquest, and establishment of an empire, as had the first voyage of Columbus.

Before we delve more deeply into results of the Dutch and British commerce in spices, or into the reasons for the value of and great demand for spices in the Middle Ages and later throughout Europe, it might be well to examine more fully the ancient spice trade conducted by the Arabs in the many centuries between the beginning of civilization in Mesopotamia and the fall of the Roman Empire.

What kept the price of pepper and other spices so high in ancient Rome, for example, was the cost of transportation from China, India, and Indonesia by the caravan routes to Europe or the Mediterranean, where it was picked up by those remarkable traders, the Phoenicians, and transported by them to the markets of the West. The Phoenicians were as canny in concealing the sources of all their trading products as the Arabs were about the origins of spices.

Because the Arabs brought the spices to the great trading centers in the Middle East, the consumers believed that "Araby" was their source, a false theory which was zealously fostered by the Arab traders. During the first years of the Roman Empire, Caesar Augustus sent an armed expedition to the Middle East to find the source of the spices and a practicable route to bring them to Rome. The Arabs misdirected the expedition and after traveling a long and hazardous journey through desolate areas it returned to Rome, empty-handed, and "unseasoned."

To appreciate the cost of spices moved by land and by sea, consider one of the most famous of the caravan routes. Spices were carried by camel from India, China, and the nearest ports of Indonesia to the Indus at Attock, just south of its junction with the Kabul River, thence through Peshawar, over the Khyber Pass, through Afganistan and Persia to Babylon on the Euphrates. The spices were then transhipped to Alexandria, or to Venice, or to Ostia, the port of Rome. There were other equally long and difficult caravan routes through Egypt. Whatever route the spices took, whether overland by camel, through the Red Sea or the Mediterranean by ship, the cost of transportation was enormous and by the time the spices reached their destination, only the wealthy could afford them. It is scant wonder that shortly before the fall of Rome and in medieval Europe spices had acquired tremendous snob appeal and become a form of currency.

After the Portuguese were driven from their possessions, their successors in the spice trade, the English and the Dutch, began the cultivation of spices in the area, increasing the yield considerably. With larger inventories and shipments in their own bottoms directly to Europe, the two competitors were gradually able to reduce the cost of spices on the open market so that they were available to people of moderate means as well as to the wealthy. (Today one wonders. Have you tried to buy Javanese pepper lately? Or Amboina cloves, or Chinese mustard, or Hungarian paprika, or Spanish saffron?)

Before the Portuguese, British, and Dutch reduced the cost of spices, the demand for them was great and the price astronomical. In Rome at one time, pepper which was much esteemed for seasoning, cost the equivalent of $200 a pound and that was Troy weight, or twelve ounces. At the height of the Empire, spices had become essential to patrician cooking. To impress their guests, the rich insisted on seasoning many of their dishes with Indonesian spices. The only surviving Roman cookbook, that of Apicius, suggests a sauce including pepper, cumin, and ginger for roast meat. The wealthy disliked or pretended to dislike simple foods and served most of their dishes with highly seasoned sauces. The demand thus created of course increased the cost, which the Romans paid mostly with barter goods such as beads, pottery, gems, and in the case of the already luxurious and wily Chinese, mostly silver and gold, which nearly bankrupted Rome.

Pepper was so valuable there in the first century A.D. that it was used as currency, being counted out, corn by corn, and was accepted in payment of taxes. Nor did the value of pepper and other spices diminish with the fall of Rome. In medieval Europe a pound of ginger would buy a sheep; three sheep or half a cow could be had for a pound of mace. In France a pound of pepper would purchase freedom for a serf. One Mediterranean customs official had a fine angle. For a bribe of a pound of pepper, he would pass any cargo, duty-free. He must have died a very rich man, unless, of course, he died at the hands of some other equally corrupt official who sought the hiding place of the pepper.

Their use in cookery was probably not, however, what created the first European demand for spices. Rather it was their medicinal properties. During classical times the Greek, Roman, and other European communities learned of the medical and gastronomic virtues of spices from returning travelers, traders, conquering armies, and fleets. The information thus brought to Europe created a demand for these products of the Orient, presumably first for the cure of diseases and later for the preservation and seasoning of food. According to what might loosely be termed an imaginary *materia medica* of the period, spices or herbs were believed to cure everything from venereal disease to softening of the brain. Each spice seems to have been thought a specific against one or another illness. Originally, in the areas where hot herbs and spices were indigenous, man learned by tasting the heat of peppercorns, the numbing and halitosis-preventing qualities of cloves, and the penetrating effectiveness of mint.

About the middle of the fourth century B.C. pepper was used only as a medicine. Cloves were valued for freshening the breath. Indeed, at that time in China no one could have an audience with the emperor without lodging a clove in his mouth. Cloves produce a highly volatile oil which has been used as a light local anesthetic— indeed it is still used by dentists for that purpose. A whole clove, held against an aching tooth was believed to, and to some degree did, alleviate pain. The oils of cloves and of cinnamon have been tested and found to be better germicides than carbolic acid.

Sage is noted not only for its aromatic odor and as seasoning for lamb and fowl, but also because it was believed to have stimulating and astringent properties. For many years sage tea was drunk in England as a home remedy for colds, and is still used there as a gargle.

Although saffron is seldom used today medicinally except as coloring matter in tinctures, it was once believed to have carminative and slight narcotic properties. Cinnamon was thought to be a tonic as well as a germicide; coriander an antiseptic; and the oils of mace and nutmeg effective in treating either renal or hepatic colic.

Garlic is a very special case. Botanists may call it an herb, but I am a cook, and I know empirically that in the culinary arts it is definitely a spice. If you doubt it has fire, try eating a clove or two raw. Garlic, which originated on the steppes of Central Asia and was later cultivated in Egypt and Syria, was used as a palliative against the effects of the sun on field laborers, and the torrid winds of the simoon. But garlic does have true medicinal properties, being rich in vitamins B, C, and D. It has long been considered a blood cleanser and is frequently eaten by people who wish to ward off colds. As colds are contagious, if you eat enough raw garlic you will probably hold anyone with a cold at breath's length, so to speak. Indeed you will probably keep everyone else at the same distance. Garlic's virtue as a seasoning agent is clearly illustrated by its constant use in the three oldest and five greatest cuisines that man is privileged to eat: Chinese, Indian, Greek, Italian, and French. Consider what any one of them would be like without garlic.

Nor do the virtues of garlic end there. Garlic was long held to be essential at any feast of Hecate's and a sovereign specific against vampires. It is still used, as a matter of fact, in those parts of the world where vampires are believed to exist. To prevent the blood-sucking creatures from entering your house you must cover all openings—doors, windows, cracks, crevices, and dog or cat doors, with festoons of garlic. The spice says to the vampire what the French said to the Germans at Verdun in 1916: "Thou shalt not pass." Furthermore, as is well known, the only way to kill a vampire is to catch him while he sleeps, fill his mouth with garlic, and drive a wooden stake through his heart. But let us return to less serious concerns, and consider the qualities of other spices.

Oregano, that favorite of Italian chefs, was once used as a cure for indigestion, but also and more important to those so wounded, as a first-aid application on spider bites and scorpion stings. If you have ever been bitten by the one or stung by the other you will realize the vital necessity of quick relief.

If, so the ancients thought, oregano cured indigestion, anise prevented it. They believed that sesame seed was a laxative, as well it may be. Mint contributes a penetrating taste wherever it is used as a seasoning and has now become an ingredient in liniments, nasal sprays, cough drops, toothpaste, and God save the mark, chewing gum. It is also, in its catnip form, much beloved of cats.

Another spice, mustard, has almost as many medical and season-ing qualities as garlic, although it has no effect on vampires, were-wolves, and other powers of darkness. Even today a poultice is made of ground mustard, flour, and water, and is applied to the chest of a patient suffering from pain in the area. The heat of the mustard is supposed to increase circulation and thus reduce the pain. As a boy I suffered under this treatment; I thought little of it then and still do. If you are aquiver to try the mustard plaster's efficacy, I believe you can still find one, ready made, at certain drug stores.

Like garlic, ginger has many virtues and a vice or two. You would be hard put to conceive of Cantonese dishes lacking the flavor of ginger, which is also a much used spice in the cuisine of the West Indies. The Chinese are of the opinion that ginger aids digestion. They and other peoples believed it has a highly aphrodisiac effect. Some—although perhaps an old mares' tale—say that certain horse breeders rub the vulvae of mares with ginger to bring them into heat before their season. About this I am no expert, but I can say that ginger as an aphrodisiac with human beings is about as effec-tive as raw oysters, or raw eggs with sherry. This is by way of saying it has no effect at all. With human beings, only cantharides (Span-ish fly to you) a deadly poison, is truly an aphrodisiac, and it is not a spice but a powder made from dead and desiccated bugs. Jacques Casanova admits using the powder for purposes less than honorable. While having no real medicinal qualities, ginger is often mixed with brandy by the British both for drinking and cooking purposes. You can consume a lot more ginger-flavored brandy (70 proof) than straight cognac (80 proof) without getting drunk. Perhaps, after all, this is a medicinal effect.

Aside from the physical and medicinal properties mentioned, cer-tain spices and herbs were assumed to have psychological effects. Thyme was supposed to have an arcane power to cure shyness; basil lifts the spirits and helps the heart; the bay leaf, so much used today in stocks and sauces, was supposed to drive off evil spirits—vampires excluded—and even the grim reaper himself. With all these medici-nal qualities ascribed rightly or wrongly to spices and herbs, it is scant wonder their European value became greater than that of gold, silver, or gems; or even perhaps a piece of the True Cross as sold by a palmer just returned from the Holy Land.

Later when the preservative and food-seasoning virtues of spices became known, naturally the value of spices as a status symbol and even as a form of currency rose mightily. But even before they became a part of the cuisine, spices developed other attributes which increased the demand for them, hence their value.

Two factors other than those medicinal and gastronomic increased the demand for spices in the ancient world: religion and vanity. In addition to frankincense and myrrh, the resins which formed the basis for much temple incense, a number of spices were used in rites to praise the constantly proliferating pantheon of deities, by the priests who performed these rites, to purify the temples in which the gods were worshipped. Many faiths, especially those of Egypt, required the embalming of the dead, and in some areas spices played an important part in this process.

From the earliest times until today both men and women have used cosmetics to make their appearances, they think, more attractive. Nero and Caligula are notorious examples; so too we are told, was Cleopatra. Spices were frequently used in compounding these lotions, eye shadows, lip salves, and powders.

Of probably greater importance was the use of the sweet and pleasant smelling oils derived from spices in the making of perfumes and toilet waters. From the beginning of the Dark Ages, circa 475 A.D., through the Middle Ages, the Renaissance, and indeed, down to the middle of the nineteenth century, bathing was not the popular everyday occupation it has become. As a matter of fact, according to Dr. Johnson's dictum to Mrs. Thrale, people "stank." Unblessed by the antiperspirants and deodorants of today, people turned to strong scents made from unguents, many of which included various spices, to conceal their body odors.

Each of these nongustatory demands for spices naturally increased their value so that by 408 A.D. when Alaric brought his Visigoths before the walls of Rome, part of the ransom he demanded for not storming and sacking the city was 3,000 pounds of pepper. Two years later when he and his followers again arrived at Rome, he apparently had run out of pepper and the Romans had no more to offer him. In any case he stormed, took, and sacked the city.

The next great European demand for spices and other luxuries of the Middle and the Far East was created by the Crusades. Those religious wars in which Christendom sought to free the holy city of Jerusalem from Islam, and incidentally carve out new principalities for many of the leaders and highly placed nobles of the invading armies, lasted almost 200 years. The first, or Peoples Crusade, organized by Pope Urban II in 1095 A.D. included some 300,000 souls led by Godfrey of Bouillon and ended in the capture of Jerusalem, of which Godfrey was made king. The following seven crusades were less successful and ended in the loss of Jerusalem to the Saracens who also took Acre in 1291 A.D., driving the last of the Christians out of the Holy Land. During the two centuries from the first to the eighth Crusade, hundreds of thousands of Frenchmen, Italians, Englishmen, Spaniards, and Germans, whose lives and diets at home immediately after the Dark Ages could only be called barbaric by comparison with the lives of the citizens of Damascus, Baghdad, and Jerusalem, were exposed to the luxuries and noble cuisines of the East.

It is a fact of history that barbarian conquerors of a civilized country which they occupy, are in turn themselves conquered by the niceties and gracious living of the civilization they have over-thrown. While the semibarbaric Europeans never really conquered the Moslems, they did capture and occupy for decades many Islamic cities and towns which were as much renowned for their splendor and high living standards as the cities of far Cathay. The men of England, Wales, and Scotland; of Normandy, Burgundy, and Provence; of Navarre, Galicia, and Catalonia; of Flanders; of Pisa, Genoa, Venice, and Siena; and of the Teutonic towns, enjoyed what to them must have been unheard-of comfort and unbelievable fare. Those who returned to their homes demanded the same style of living they had enjoyed as unwelcome guests of their Moslem hosts. The Crusades did not free the Holy Land, but they civilized those who sought to free it. Once again the Franks returned home and demanded pepper, saffron, nutmeg, cinnamon, and ginger for culinary purposes.

Marco Polo, however, did not return to Venice from China until four years after the fall of Acre, and his memoirs, containing the sources of various spices, were not known in Europe until well into the fourteenth century. Meanwhile the Arabs dominated the spice trade, although it was now Venice and Genoa which carried these valuable cargoes through the Mediterranean. Another 100 years would pass before Vasco da Gama brought the first shipment of spices from their origin to Portugal.

In addition to their pharmaceutical and cosmetic virtues, spices have two others, both gastronomic, which contributed highly to the demand for them throughout the western world both before the fall of Rome and after the Crusades. Spices, especially the peppers, could act as a preservative for meat and fish; and the more tangy spices could mask the taste of bad food. Other spices could alleviate nausea caused by bad water. One of the major concerns of chefs from the Middle Ages to about 1860 was to disguise rancidity of spoiling foods—nothing could conceal actual putrefaction. The more fiery or pungent the spice or spices, mostly the more expensive ones, the more effectively they concealed the flavor of food which was either of poor quality in the first place or had begun to go bad. As one gastronomic pundit once remarked: "All food in the Middle Ages was middle-aged, verging on senility; what wasn't, was too young to be weaned from its mother. In either case it required a spicy sauce to be edible."

When I first heard that spices could be used to preserve food, rather than conceal the taste of viands that were tainted, I had my doubts. They were completely resolved by a conversation with an internist at the National Naval Medical Center in Bethesda, Maryland. Dr. Joseph Cassells told me that the bacteria which causes the food to spoil could be held at bay by the use of hot spices, especially pepper. The latter acted more or less like refrigeration in reverse. Low temperatures either killed or retarded the growth of bacteria; hot spices created what Dr. Cassells called "an incompatible culture medium," which seems to discourage the proliferation of germs. Such scientific testimony seemed conclusive, but further research adduced other facts.

Until 1816, when they were stamped out by the combined efforts of the United States and Royal navies, pirates had their bases on the Spanish Main, the coastal strip between Panama and the mouth of the Orinoco River. From these bases maritime outlaws brought rapine, rape, and murder to all shipping, especially the Spanish plate ships, crossing the Caribbean. These pirates, who had the first completely integrated society as far as race, color, creed, and sex, preserved their meat in spices. No salt pork for the gentlemen-adventurers who sailed under the Jolly Roger. Their meat, mostly wild boar, was first smoked and then treated with allspice from Jamaica so that they dined better than most mariners of the times. It is interesting to note that meat thus treated was known as "boucan" which evolved through the lingua franca of the coast into "bouca-neer." That word eventually became "buccaneer," a euphemistic term for pirate. The moral of this instructive little incident is to show that spices, the basis of fiery food, not only affected trade for centuries, brought about the discovery of the New World, created new principalities and empires, but also contributed to the development of the English language. Other such examples are the words "grocer" and "grocery." They derive directly from "grossarie," men in charge of the *peso grosso*, the great beam scales, who were responsible in England for detecting and preventing the adulteration of pepper and other spices, especially that most expensive of all, saffron. At one time the adulteration of saffron, like other and more fervid kinds of adultery, was punished by death.

It is clear from all the foregoing that spices and the search for them have had enormous effects on the entire civilized, and, at times, the uncivilized world. Indeed, they became one of man's most cherished and sought-after possessions. Should you wish to pursue the history of their use in cooking you will find much additional lore on medieval and renaissance kitchen techniques and recipes in *The Delectable Past*, by Esther B. Aresty, and *A Fifteenth Century Cookery Book*, by John L. Anderson. For Roman cookery the recently reprinted English edition of the previously mentioned Apicius is about the only source. All are available in book shops which cater to the taste—in both senses of the word—of culinary or gastronomic cognoscenti.

We now come to consider what I think is the most interesting and enlightening subject connected with fiery food: why is it part of the daily diet of people who live in tropical climes?

I was brought up in Baltimore whose climate in summer is more tropical than that of the Philippines, at least so I have been told by military personnel stationed at both places. My first experience with the use of hot food in hot weather was really my wife's. During a hot spell—temperature range 85 to 100 degrees for ten consecutive days and no air conditioning—we had been living almost exclusively on cold food: cold cuts, salads, and so forth. My wife came down with what is usually an unpleasant but transitory intestinal complaint. After several days of malaise, she consulted her physician who warned her against an exclusive diet of cold food in hot weather. He prescribed at least one hot meal each day. Following his regimen, she recovered. Mrs. C.'s recovery led me into the logical fallacy of *post hoc ergo propter hoc*. I assumed that hot food in hot weather was essential; I also confused physically hot with chemically hot dishes. One other experience in Baltimore, however, tended to confirm my theory. On this particular night, the outside temperature was approximately 97 degrees Fahrenheit. Only the weather bureau knew the humidity. My friends and I, sweating at every pore, ate an extremely good and reasonably fiery curry. It seemed to me as we sat afterwards on the stoop in front of the host's house, that I felt much cooler than I had before the meal, although a check of the thermometer disclosed no drop in temperature. On the basis of these two events I conceived the theory, which had some merit as I later learned, that if you raised the temperature inside your body to equal that outside, you would be more comfortable.

Despite all this empirical knowledge I consulted experts. Taking advantage of my situation here in Washington, I talked to biochemists, physicians, and dieticians at the National Naval Medical Center, as well as the Walter Reed Army Medical Center, the National Academy of Sciences, and the National Institutes of Health. I asked all my correspondents the same question. "People living in hot climates invariably eat hot food. Why?" As you might expect, answers from the experts seemed to vary. But carefully analyzed, they all said much the same thing.

The first reply I had to my question came as a kind of shock. It was the same answer given by a famous mountain climber when asked why he risked his life to scale a most dangerous peak. "Because it's there." "They eat fiery food," said my informant "because it's there." Which is undeniable since chili peppers, for example, have been cultivated in Central America since at least 5000 B.C. (In this connection it is worthy to note how the spice trade fed on itself, so to speak. Chili peppers, now used in curries, were unknown in the Far East until the Portuguese introduced them into India from Brazil during the sixteenth century.)

The second and more responsive answer to my question amplified the first. Dr. T. D. Boaz of the National Institute of Sciences pointed out that not only were hot spices indigenous to hot countries but so, too, were the staples of their several diets. In the Americas the staple was maize; in India, the Spice Islands, south China, and Malaysia it was rice; and in north China, especially Szechuan province whence Marco Polo brought pasta to Italy, wheat. All three of these foods were, he explained, high in starch and very bland to the taste. Along with them grew the spices, which, judiciously mixed with the staple, made it not only edible but appetizing. Thus through trial and error over the centuries came the sophisticated cuisines of the Far and Middle East, of China, and the northern parts of Latin America. A famous example of this admixture of bland and fiery local food comes from a Mexican dish, probably invented by the Aztecs, and frequently served today with cocktails. It is guacamole—a combination of two bland ingredients: tomatoes and avocados; and fiery chili peppers. Depending on the recipe it can be bland enough for children or strong enough to destroy the taste buds of an adult.

I had more and, to me, very consoling data from the National Institutes of Health, where Dr. John Seal confirmed my opinion about the effect of equalizing the interior and exterior heat of the body. He said that the intake of fiery food raised the interior body temperature, opened the pores and made you glow if you were a woman, perspire if you were a man, and lather if you were a horse. In any case opening of the pores and resultant evaporation of liquid tends to make you feel cool, just as many electric refrigerators cool their contents by evaporation.

Another item of interest I learned: fiery food, like alcohol, is habit-forming. If you accustom yourself to neat whiskey, you will never again be completely satisfied with watered strong waters; once you have acquired a taste for fiery food you will never again be satisfied with bland fare. After you have eaten even a moderately fiery chicken curry, you will never again be completely satisfied with chicken à la king. All of this is neatly summed up by a couple of lines from a verse attributed to Rudyard Kipling: "If the wife of the Vicar has never touched liquor, Look out when she finds the Champagne."

In all candor I must confess that one of my consultants disagreed with his colleagues. He said he had spent a good part of his service in World War II studying the diet of American soldiers and sailors in the southwest Pacific, and concluded they would be healthier on a regimen of salads and cold viands than on the local dishes. I prefer to be guided by the consensus of his confreres. He sounds too much like a xenophobic major I knew who believed that even Roman water should be boiled before being drunk, and that French cheese was dangerous because the milk had not been pasteurized. I am sure he never suffered a gastric complaint; I am equally sure he never enjoyed a decent meal.

But let us leave the major to his unenviable fate and get on with the following recipes to learn just how good fiery food can be.

CANAPÉS AND HORS D'OEUVRE

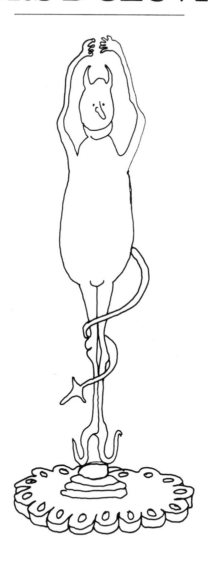

$\mathbf{A}$ll canapés are hors d'oeuvre; not all hors d'oeuvre are canapés. In general small canapés are crackers or pieces of toast covered with a paté or spread of some kind, or holding a small bit of sausage, a shrimp, a sardine, cheese, et cetera. Usually served cold, canapés are sometimes hot: chicken livers wrapped in bacon and tiny Swedish meatballs are examples. While, strictly speaking, dips do not fit the definition of canapés because they are not served on toast or crackers, but with potato, rice, or maize chips, custom and usage have made them part of the canapé family. Canapés are served with drinks before a meal and at cocktail parties. They are never a course at a luncheon, dinner, or supper. Another distinction between canapés and other hors d'oeuvre is that the former are almost always eaten with the fingers or toothpicks, whereas other hors d'oeuvre, served at table as a course either preceding or immediately following the soup, are eaten with flat silver. You may have a half dozen or more canapés with your preprandial drinks; you will rarely have more than one other kind of hors d'oeuvre at a seated meal. And you very rarely have canapés before a meal if your menu calls for another kind of hors d'oeuvre at the meal itself.

Hors d'oeuvre served as a course can be either hot or cold. Antipasto is a fine example of the latter; baked stuffed mushrooms of the former.

Cerealia

ABOUT 18 CUPS

Cerealia is an invented name for a cereal-based cocktail snack, which can be bought under various trade names in quart jars, but for a price. Making it yourself you not only save money but can regulate the seasoning. I suspect that the original inventor of the commercial variety held stock in a large cereal company, as well as in a distillery and a brewery. Few other cocktail canapés are so thirst inducing.

Like some revolvers, Cerealia has a double action. It has "the blotting-paper effect," as it absorbs a fairly high percentage of the alcohol it induces you to consume, thus warding off or delaying intoxication. The other attribute it shares with salted almonds, popcorn, and olives: it is habit-forming. Once you start eating it you find yourself hooked and go on munching so long as any remains.

Salted almonds, popcorn, and olives depend on salt to induce thirst; Cerealia depends on garlic. This herb, along with a sprinkling of cayenne, makes Cerealia a much more fiery and sprightly comestible than the other three. I am indebted to Signorina Carettaio for experimenting with Cerealia until she worked out the proper proportions of garlic and cayenne. May her shadow never grow less.

4 cups Rice Chex	2 tablespoons celery salt
6 cups "spoon-sized" shredded wheat	4 teaspoons cayenne
4 cups Cheerios	3 tablespoons Worcestershire sauce
4 cups pretzel sticks	½ teaspoon Tabasco
1 pound butter	1 cup Spanish peanuts
3 tablespoons garlic salt	
1 tablespoon garlic powder	

Preheat the oven to 250 degrees and place the first 4 ingredients in the largest available shallow baking pan. Melt the butter and mix the spices into it. Add the Worcestershire and Tabasco. Pour over the cereal mixture and mix thoroughly. Bake covered for about an hour, stirring frequently. Add the peanuts, uncover, and bake another 30 minutes, or until crisp. Cool and store in jars.

Guacamole Pancho Villa

1 QUART

Among the unknowing who live north of the southern border of the United States an impression exists that all Mexican food is fiery. A cookbook has been written to allay this impression and to prove that Mexican food is actually mostly bland. I cannot completely agree. Chili peppers and chili powder are grown and made in the land of the Toltecs and Mayas. Both kinds of chili are used in most Mexican cooking. Some Mexican cooking, therefore, must be as fiery as the señoritas.

Guacamole, a famous and often-served dip at cocktail parties, can be either bland or fiery. This recipe came to me indirectly from one Señor Arango Zapata who claimed to have ridden with the notorious partisan leader. Whether you follow the Zapata recipe or use a blander version of Guacamole, eschew serving salty crackers or potato chips with it. Toasted tortillas or tostados make the ideal accompaniment.

1 medium ripe tomato	A good grinding of black
1 medium onion	pepper
2 medium ripe avocados	1 teaspoon dried sweet
3 tablespoons fresh	basil
lemon juice	6 healthy dashes Tabasco
1½ teaspoons crushed	2 tablespoons
dried red chili peppers	mayonnaise
1 teaspoon salt	

Peel tomato, remove seeds and weedy parts. Mince pulp and set aside. Mince onion and set aside. Peel avocados and cut into chunks. Place chunks in a mixing bowl and immediately add lemon juice to prevent avocado from turning an unappetizing dirty brownish green. Mash avocado well with a fork. Add chili peppers, salt, black pepper, basil, Tabasco, and mayonnaise to avocado bowl. Mix well with the fork. Now put in the minced tomato and onion. Mix again, and put guacamole in refrigerator to chill at least 4 hours.

Serve at room temperature. As with most hot dishes the fiery effect is not apparent for several seconds after you have eaten it: at first taste it is soft and smooth, *then* comes the backlash.

The George Anson Canapé

1 CANAPÉ

Only a naval historian could recognize the value of Admiral George, Baron Anson to the Royal Navy. But you do not have to be a naval expert to recognize the value of the George Anson Canapé as an accompaniment to drinks. If you have the proper ingredients, it is probably the easiest of all canapés to make. I found it on the S.S. *George Anson,* a cargo vessel plying between Australia, the Philippines, Hong Kong, Japan, Taiwan, Guam, and Fiji.

Promptly at 12 M. and at 6 P.M., the Chinese bar steward placed on each table a bowl of groundnuts or goobers, and a plate of the ship's specialty: The George Anson Canapé. The bowl was kept full; the plate was seldom replenished. Naturally, the canapés disappeared with celerity. You will come to understand this phenomenon.

The canapés are not fiery fiery, but do induce a thirst which seems best succored by dry martinis, pink gins, or Scotch whiskey.

Your only problem will be to find the proper ingredients: sharp cheddar cheese and preserved ginger. For this canapé you must have the sharpest possible cheddar cheese as well as preserved ginger that is about the size of golf balls and is put up in extremely light, not too sweet syrup. You can probably find this kind of ginger in oriental grocery stores or markets. The Canton ginger used in many desserts is much too sweet.

Preserved ginger, as above	*1 round, colored, cocktail*
1 half-inch cube sharp	*toothpick*
cheddar cheese	

Drain ginger, reserving the jar for use as a flower vase. Wash ginger in cold running water to remove any lingering syrup, dry between paper towels, and cut into ½-inch cubes. Pierce a ginger cube in the center with a toothpick and push the ginger down the shaft until ½ inch of wood sticks out. Impale a ½-inch cheese cube with the end of the toothpick and you have a George Anson Canapé. The more colors your toothpicks, the better show the platter will make.

The Mephistophelian Mushroom

1 QUART

Candor compels me to confess that I adapted this recipe from an original blandish recipe of mine.

When I was a youth I saw through a glass darkly and became interested in the secret, black, and midnight arts. I longed, vainly of course, to study under Hecate, the Queen of the Witches, and became a wizard. Ever since I have had a beneficent—if that be the proper adjective—feeling for the three M's: Machiavelli, Merlinus, and Mephistopheles. Hence, when it came to naming this dish, I thought of these three, the greatest of whom is Mephistopheles.

Making the mushrooms is an assembly-line process, but you should allow at least three days from production to eating that they may marinate properly. You should start with sterilized, wide-mouthed jars with tight-fitting lids.

3 eight-ounce cans fancy button mushrooms	¾ cup olive oil
5 medium garlic cloves	1 tablespoon salt
4 large dried red chili peppers	2 teaspoons Tabasco
4 tablespoons red wine vinegar	2 tablespoons lemon pepper marinade
	1 teaspoon cracked red pepper

Drain the mushrooms through a colander. While mushrooms drain, peel garlic and cut into thirds. Cut dried chili peppers in half. Place vinegar, olive oil, salt, Tabasco, lemon pepper marinade, and cracked red pepper in a bowl and blend well. Set aside.

Cover bottom of jar with 2 layers of mushrooms. Add 2 pieces of garlic and another 2 layers of mushrooms. Evenly spaced around the jar, insert upright against the glass 4 of the halved chili peppers. Add 3 layers of mushrooms and 3 pieces of garlic. Arrange the remaining halves of red chili peppers as you did the first. Add the last of the garlic and fill the jar with the rest of the mushrooms.

Stir contents of bowl vigorously until they are fully integrated and pour over the mushrooms. Fill to the top with the marinade. Cover the jar tightly, using a Gilhoolie jar opener in reverse to make the jar as tight as possible. Set jar upside down for 12 hours to marinate the top mushrooms. Reverse jar and let stand for another 12 hours. Continue this process for at least another day. The mushrooms will then be sufficiently marinated to eat. They will be better if they stand on tops or bottoms for another 2 days, and will keep for at least 3 weeks. *Never* refrigerate. Shake jar well and drain mushrooms before serving.

Sands' Moon Shots

20 CRACKERS

Hal Sands is a friend who used to live in the Valley of the Moon, California. In addition to his many other talents, he made various kinds of chutney, and also perfected this splendid canapé. Extremely simple, it has the additional merit of longevity. After the moon shots are made they may be stored almost indefinitely in an airtight container. A further plus is that they may be served hot immediately as they are done, or cold at a later date. In either case they make a fiery canapé well suited to any kind of cocktail.

About the only edible, if it is edible at all, worse than wet bread, is a wet cracker, which is how this canapé starts. Be not put off. Wet crackers are the first step only. I have a thing against Saltines per se, but when treated in the Sands manner they lose their original character and become a joy for as long as they last, which will not be long.

20 Saltines	1 tablespoon oregano
½ cup (1 stick) melted butter	1 tablespoon poppy seeds
2 tablespoons curry powder	

Preheat the oven to 200 degrees. Place Saltines 1 inch apart in a shallow pan. Add small quantity of water, but not enough to cover Saltines. After they have absorbed water and expanded, brush each lightly with melted butter. Sprinkle them with curry powder, oregano, and poppy seeds. Place in the preheated oven for about 1½ hours. Remove from oven. Serve at once or store until needed.

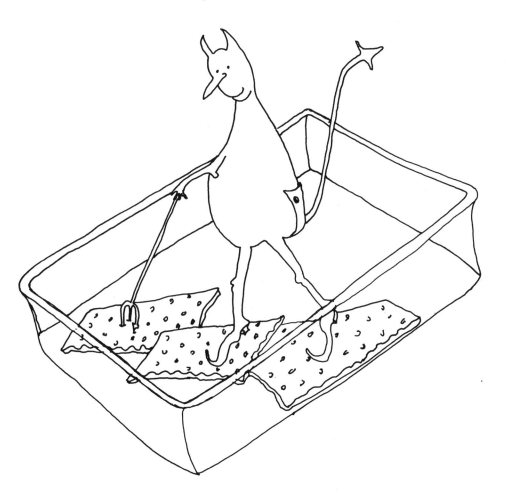

Shrimp Shaitan

ABOUT 24 SHRIMP

Shaitan is an Arabic word meaning "the evil one." The diabolical difficulty of these shrimp is that you never have enough. Despite their undoubted messiness, they are always more popular than cleaned shrimp dipped in a sauce.

A problem which may rear its ugly head is finding the chief spicy ingredient: Old Bay Seasoning. It is made in Baltimore and I doubt it can be bought throughout the United States. All is not lost. Get a jar of mixed pickling spice. It has almost the same ingredients as Old

Bay Seasoning. The latter is a powder and the former must be ground, if not into a powder, at least into smaller particles than those in the jar.

After the shrimp are cooked as below, put them in the refrigerator until cold. To serve, place them unshelled, on a napkin on a silver salver. The fact that each of your guests has to shell his own shrimp will reduce the intake, and each guest will feel as though he had done a day's work. Be sure that you provide many paper napkins with the shrimp. Finger bowls with hot water and slices of lemon would not be amiss.

1 tablespoon Old Bay Sea- *soning or mixed pickling* *spice*	*2 teaspoons cayenne* *½ teaspoon poppy seeds* *½ teaspoon celery seeds*
1 teaspoon salt *½ cup lemon juice*	*1 pound raw shrimp*

Mix well in a small bowl all ingredients except shrimp. Add ¼ cup water and mix again. Place raw, unshelled shrimp in a heavy sauce-pan. Cover with the mixture and stir well. Place the saucepan, covered, over medium heat. Bring to a boil. Reduce heat and simmer 20 minutes. Drain, and cool as above.

Deviled Eggs

3 OR 4 EGGS

The deviled egg provided by caterers and home economists for cocktail accompaniments is a pallid and insipid comestible compared with this article. Designed and perfected by a charming female fiend, whom I count as friend, these deviled eggs seem to have come out of the back door of Hell. Actually the eggs are not all that fiery, but they definitely have verve. The secret is the use of mustard instead of mayonnaise as a binding agent.

Friends of my friendly fiend planned a surprise birthday party for her on a canal barge but they ran into gastronomic difficulties. They had to call on the birthday girl for help. This she provided. One of her contributions was 98 deviled eggs; I suspect she has three hands. During their preparation, she made up a few experimental samples for me. Several of us tried her versions and decided that the following recipe definitely belonged.

¾ teaspoon dry mustard
½ teaspoon distilled white
   vinegar
1 teaspoon prepared hot
   horseradish

1 tablespoon deviled ham
2 hard-boiled eggs
Paprika

In a small bowl mix the mustard with the vinegar. Be sure there are no lumps and let the mixture stand for about 10 minutes to set. Mix the horseradish with the ham and add the mustard which should by now be about 1 teaspoon of mustard paste. Remove the yolks of 2 eggs and mash these into the mixture, being sure all is well incorporated. Fill 3 of the hard egg whites with generous portions of the mixture and garnish with a light sprinkling of paprika. If you are frugal, fill all 4 egg white halves with the mixture. The effect will not be so splendid, but it will suffice. Serve eggs cold, of course.

The Horseradish Sandwich

18 SANDWICHES

In my presalad days, I frequently met my father, mother, and sister at the Rennert in Baltimore for dinner. Usually I was there ahead of them. My mother had no sense of time. I was hungry, naturally, and I soon discovered that a discreetly raised eyebrow at the head waiter, who had known my father for years, would produce a plate of rolls, butter, and a jar of horseradish. It was then I discovered that fiery food was desirable. I often ate a whole plate of rolls, and a jar of horseradish while waiting. Hence this horseradish sandwich which I have refined over the years.

The first refinement was to use oysterettes instead of rolls. The second was to make a three-decker. This you can still do in restaurants if you order raw oysters or clams. You then get a kind of elaborate salver on which is a bowl of oyster crackers, a bottle of Tabasco, and a jar of horseradish. Seizing a cracker in your left hand you place a small bit of butter on it; you cover this with another cracker, and add to that about half again as much horseradish. This you top with a third cracker. Then pop the whole shaky structure into your mouth. For the purposes of this book I have devised a much more stable sandwich which will not fall apart and can be prepared in quantity well ahead of the cocktails. For this you will need the commercial so-called beaten biscuit. The small flat fairly hard biscuits come in packages of 36.

*1 tablespoon unsalted
  butter*
*2 tablespoons prepared
  hot horseradish*

*36 commercial beaten
  biscuits*

Place butter in a small bowl and let it become malleable. Add horseradish and mix the ingredients with a fork or spoon until they have become one. Now place ½ teaspoon of the mixture on a biscuit. Cover with another biscuit, and you have the horseradish sandwich. Put a few of these on your table and watch them vanish like ghosts.

Anne's Quail Eggs

30 EGGS

To my shame I remember almost nothing about Anne except her eggs and that otherwise she could not cook worth a damn. I do recall her telling me that the eggs were from an old, secret family recipe handed down from mother to daughter. As Anne told me all this at her cocktail party when she gave me the recipe, things are still a bit hazy in my mind. I remember she hinted that she was breaking the family tradition of silence on the eggs because she had had a row with her mother. Regardless of the origin of the recipe, the eggs are delicious, and quite different from the preceding deviled eggs. The ingredients may seem many. Let that not deter you, the recipe is simple and the results are as unusual as they are delectable.

Quail eggs can be purchased at any fancy grocery shop. They come hard-boiled, shelled, and fifteen to a can.

*2 five-and-one-half-ounce
  cans of quail eggs*
1 medium onion
6 tablespoons butter
*1 teaspoon cracked black
  pepper*
*½ teaspoon ground
  cinnamon*
*½ teaspoon ground
  turmeric*

1 teaspoon garlic powder
¾ teaspoon ground ginger
*¼ teaspoon ground opium
  (optional)*
*½ teaspoon ground
  coriander*
½ teaspoon ground cumin
¾ teaspoon dry mustard
¼ teaspoon cayenne
1 teaspoon curry powder

Drain quail eggs. Chop onion coarsely. Melt 4 tablespoons butter in a skillet, put in onion and cook over a low heat, stirring now and then, until onion is soft and translucent. Remove and discard onion. Meanwhile place all other ingredients except eggs, remaining butter, and curry powder into a small bowl and mix well.

Heat remaining butter in a skillet and sprinkle in the curry powder; cook it slowly, stirring to prevent burning. While curry powder cooks, spread the condiment mixture from the bowl evenly over wax paper. When the curry powder is brown, remove skillet from heat, and roll each egg in the curried butter. Then roll eggs in the condiment mixture, coating them well.

Baroque Snails

SERVES 4

This recipe comes from a fine New York restaurant, The Baroque. The recipe is simpler than it appears but does take time.

Snails belong to several menu categories. One snail on a small toast round is a canapé; six on larger rounds of toast become a first course. Use them as you will, they make an almost perfect dish for the beginning of a meal. Indeed, in larger quantities they are a good dish for a supper main course.

These snails must marinate for 72 hours. Three steps are involved: marination, heating the snails, and making the sauce. The marinade is composed of:

½ medium onion, chopped	½ teaspoon dried thyme
½ carrot, chopped	6 juniper berries
½ celery rib, chopped	6 black peppercorns
1 bay leaf	2 cups red Burgundy
1 whole clove	1 can (24) prepared snails

Place everything except snails into a bowl. Wash snails well under cold running water, add them to the bowl, and stir. Cover bowl and place in refrigerator to marinate for a minimum of 3 days, disturbing them with a wooden spoon about every 10 hours. At the end of the marination period, or when you are ready to finish the snails, you will need for heating them, and for the sauce:

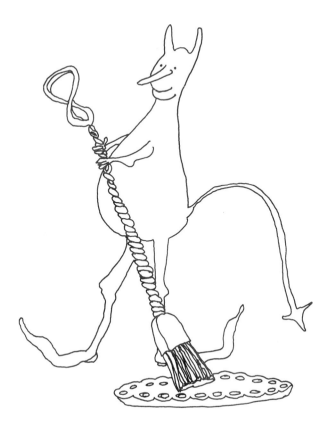

6 tablespoons butter
¾ teaspoon salt
¾ teaspoon freshly ground
    black pepper
1 teaspoon cayenne
⅓ cup cognac
9 scallions
1 large garlic clove

¼ pound fresh mushrooms
1 tablespoon minced
    parsley
1 tablespoon Worcester-
    shire sauce
4 toast rounds
4 lemon wedges

Drain snails, discarding marinade. Melt 4 tablespoons butter in a heavy skillet and add ½ teaspoon salt, ½ teaspoon black pepper, and the cayenne. When mixture is hot, add snails, stir, and simmer for 3 minutes. Add cognac and ignite. When the blue flame has burned out, place contents of skillet in the top of a double boiler over hot water and keep warm.

Mince scallions and garlic. Chop the mushrooms coarsely. Melt remaining butter in same skillet in which you cooked the snails. Add the rest of the salt and pepper, the minced scallions, garlic, parsley, chopped mushrooms, and Worcestershire sauce. Cook until scallions are soft and the mushrooms are done. Pour the sauce over the snails, heat through, and serve on toast rounds, garnishing each plate with a lemon wedge.

Maidenhead Mushrooms

SERVES 4

A number of years ago my friend Peterkin Pepit was staying in his Chelsea flat and for reasons of his own, went up the Thames to Maidenhead. It isn't far from London. At a pub called The Fouled Anchor he found a version of this dish, served as a savoury after the evening meal. He decided it would be more appropriate as a first course, rather than the last. When he returned from his trip, he and his chef, Perigord, worked it over and came up with this hors d'oeuvre.

The mushrooms should be uniform size and about 2 or 2½ inches in diameter. The stilton should be mature and hard enough to grate. For that purpose I suggest a Mouli grater rather than the old-fashioned flat grater, which you will have to use with the onion.

8 mushrooms	2 tablespoons curry
Butter	powder
¼ pound stilton cheese	1 tablespoon ground
½ medium onion	cumin seed
2 lemons	Fine bread crumbs
¼ cup sour cream	1 pimento
1 tablespoon Worcester-	
shire sauce	

Stem and wash mushrooms; dry between towels. Melt 5 tablespoons butter in a heavy skillet, add mushrooms, and cook until they are brown but still firm, turning from time to time to cook both tops and bottoms. Discard any liquid remaining in pan. While mushrooms cook, grate cheese to make 1 cup. Place in a bowl. Grate onion and add to cheese. Squeeze lemons and add juice to bowl. Pour in sour cream. Add Worcestershire sauce, curry powder, and cumin. Mix well. Taste and add additional cheese, Worcestershire, or sour cream, if needed. If mixture is not sufficiently fiery, a few dashes of Tabasco could be included, but will hardly be required.

After mushrooms have cooked let them cool and fill centers with the mixture from the bowl. About 5 minutes before you are ready to serve, sprinkle mushrooms lightly with bread crumbs, dot with butter and place under a hot broiler flame until the crumbs brown, about 3 minutes. Meanwhile, cut pimento into 16 strips about 1½ inches long and ⅛ inch wide. Garnish the finished mushrooms with the strips of pimento, crossed on top.

Maidenhead Mushrooms is an hors d'oeuvre with which you should serve wine. Pepit always preferred a nonpretentious but gratifying red Bordeaux called Château Maillard.

The Czar's Capsicum

SERVES 4

In the days when there was a Czar of all the Russias, these stuffed peppers were a favorite dish for starting a royal meal. Despite its lofty origin, this hors d'oeuvre is one we can all enjoy at little expense unless you insist on fresh caviar from the Caspian. I use lumpfish or Icelandic caviar. Both are a mite salty, but serve the purpose. Whatever kind of caviar you use—it must not be red from the salmon—you can pretend you are dining with royalty.

1½ cups cooked white kidney beans	¼ teaspoon cracked black pepper
2 large green bell peppers	3 tablespoons caviar
1 tablespoon olive oil	1 tablespoon fresh lemon juice
¼ teaspoon cracked red pepper	2 large red radishes

Preheat the oven to 275 degrees.

Place beans in a colander to drain. Run cold water through them to remove all juices. While beans drain, cut peppers in half. Being careful not to cut through the skin or bottom, remove all seeds and membranes. Almost fill a 2-quart saucepan with water, bring to a boil, and put in peppers. Boil slowly, uncovered, for 5 minutes. Remove pepper halves and drain. Put beans into a bowl and add all other ingredients, except radishes. Stir contents until all is well blended.

Fill pepper halves with contents of bowl. Place peppers on a pie plate or other flat pan and put in the preheated oven for about 5 minutes, or until peppers and contents are warm. While peppers warm, shred radishes or cut them into roses. When peppers are ready, garnish with 1 radish each and serve at once.

A chilled Rhine wine complements the peppers. For those who find them too fiery, hot, buttered French bread will act admirably as a fire extinguisher. On the other hand, if you find the dish not fiery enough, the cure is simple: add an additional ¼ teaspoon of both red and black cracked pepper to the mixture.

Peppered Tomatoes

SERVES 4

The original of this recipe is purported to have been brought to Spain by one of the followers of Pizarro. It was given to me by an archaeologist who also supplied the translation. Either the translation was inadequate or the recipe must have been intended to make a sacrificial dish for some Inca god of fire. After considerable experimentation in the kitchen, I succeeded in reducing the flames to embers and thus made it a laudable dish for the human gullet and stomach. The tomatoes are still as fiery as the furnace of Shadrach, Meshach, and Abednego, but the dish is highly satisfactory to the brazen-throated gourmet. Try it, you may like it.

1 red bell pepper	¼ cup milk
1 yellow bell pepper	1 garlic clove
¼ green bell pepper	1 teaspoon arrowroot
1 green chili pepper	¼ cup bread crumbs
1 dried red chili pepper	2 tomatoes
¼ cup mayonnaise	Salt
1 teaspoon freshly grated	Butter
or powdered horseradish	

Split peppers, remove seeds and membranes. Dice bell peppers and place in a bowl. Thinly slice green chili pepper and toss slices into the bowl. Mince the red chili pepper, discard half the seeds and let the red chili pepper follow the green into the pepper bowl. Set aside. Place mayonnaise in another bowl. Add milk and horseradish. Peel and mince garlic, put in same bowl with mayonnaise. Add arrowroot and bread crumbs and stir well to make a thick mixture. Pour contents of second bowl into the first, and, with a fork, make a smooth blend of the contents of both bowls. Allow the blend to rest while you prepare the tomatoes.

Cut the tomatoes in half and remove the pulp without breaking the skin. The best implement is a grapefruit knife. (Reserve pulp for future use in salads or stewed tomatoes.) Wash interior of tomato shells and let drain. When dry, fill tomatoes with the mixture from the bowl. Pack it well and season lightly with salt. Dot with butter. Put tomatoes on a broiling pan and place pan under low flame to heat through, about 6 minutes. Increase flame and broil 1 minute, and serve.

The fire inherent to this dish suggests that each tomato half be served on toast; or that buttered warm small pumpernickel slices accompany the tomatoes. Half a tomato per person is adequate.

Chitomion

SERVES 4

Chitomion is a portmanteau word which stands for chicken, tomato, and onion. Like many great discoveries, scientific and culinary, it was concocted by accident, largely by Rosemary, my amanuensis. We were working on a fiery vegetable dish based on onions and tomatoes. The day was murky and ill-beset. Work in the kitchen was going badly when my wife walked in and asked: "What's for lunch?" I wish I had asked first, thus shifting the problem to her. Rosemary, bless her, observed we could use the hodgepodge of tomatoes and onions if we added chicken to it. No sooner said than done, to coin a phrase. We found some leftover, cooked chicken breast in the refrigerator; and, voilà, we had a lunch. As a midday meal it was less than divine. But with a few changes we found it made a heavenly, hot—in both senses of the word—hors d'oeuvre.

Unless you have small, individual, ovenproof ramekins, you will do well to finish the hors d'oeuvre in a casserole and serve it either on toast rounds or in small pastry shells.

1 large onion	½ teaspoon salt
3 large garlic cloves	2 teaspoons dark brown
1½ tablespoons peanut oil	sugar
1 tablespoon lemon juice	1 chicken breast, cooked
6 large tomatoes	Butter
2 medium leeks	Bread crumbs
2 long green chili	
peppers	

Peel and mince onion and garlic. Put peanut oil in a large heavy skillet over a moderate flame. When hot add onion, garlic, and lemon juice. Cook, turning now and then to keep from burning. Meanwhile skin tomatoes, cut off tops, and remove seeds and pulp, either with a knife or by squeezing the tomatoes. Chop the tomatoes. Wash leeks thoroughly and slice them fine. Finely slice chili peppers. Add tomatoes, leeks, and peppers to skillet. Mix well and cook about 2 minutes. Season with salt and brown sugar. Mix well again, and simmer the whole about 10 minutes. Chop chicken breast into large dice. Mix into the contents of skillet and simmer, uncovered, for about 5 minutes to reduce liquid and heat the whole thoroughly.

Grease with butter the individual ramekins or the casserole, and pour in the contents of skillet. Sprinkle with bread crumbs and dot with butter. Three minutes before serving, place under high broiler flame to melt butter and brown bread crumbs. Serve at once. If you do the final cooking in a casserole, and plan to serve in *small* pastry shells, warm the latter before filling them. If you are serving the dish on toast rounds be sure the toast is both buttered and hot.

Artichokes Tartare

SERVES 4

Steak tartare probably dates back to the Golden Horde—the Mongols who, under Batu Khan, ravaged Europe as far as Pešht in the thirteenth century. I added the artichoke bottoms which come in cans. They should be about 2½ inches in diameter, raw, and packed in light brine or water.

8 *artichoke bottoms*
½ *cup vinaigrette sauce*
¾ *pound finely ground*
   sirloin of beef
1 *teaspoon mayonnaise*
1 *egg white*
1 *tablespoon Worcester-*
   shire sauce

1 *teaspoon Tabasco*
½ *teaspoon salt*
½ *teaspoon freshly ground*
   black pepper
1 *teaspoon dry mustard*
8 *rolled anchovy fillets,*
   stuffed with capers

Wash artichoke bottoms, place in a saucepan, cover with water, and simmer until soft enough to be cut with a salad fork, about 10 minutes. While the bottoms cook make the vinaigrette sauce. Drain bottoms between towels, and refrigerate. Place all remaining ingredients except the anchovies, in a bowl and mix well. You can do this with a fork and spoon, but your fingers are better. Add vinaigrette sauce to the bowl, and mix again. Place bowl in a cool place but not in refrigerator.

About 20 minutes before you are ready to serve, place 2 artichoke bottoms on each of 4 salad plates. Divide contents of bowl among the bottoms, making each a trimly shaped, plateau-topped mound. Place a rolled anchovy on each plateau and refrigerate until you are ready to serve. The hors d'oeuvre should be chilled but not cold.

With this dish you would be well advised to present some warmed sesame-seed crackers. A soft red wine, preferably a Bordeaux, would complement the dish, and compliment your guests.

Istimewa Prawn Basket

SERVES 4

When I was last in Hong Kong, friends took us to a Malaysian restaurant called Istimewa, which means "excellent." The restaurant, owned and run by Madame Kwek, lives up to its name. Our host, a Crown Colony judge, immediately asked if we could start our meal with the "little prawn baskets." We did. The baskets were exactly that, woven out of pie pastry, filled with a combination of chopped shrimp, finely sliced chili peppers, and coarsely chopped parsley. I persuaded Madame Kwek to part with the recipe.

Either you know how to make pie pastry—or you don't. If you do, no problem. If you do not, substitute small prepared patty shells, about 2½ inches in diameter. The filling for the shells, as Madame Kwek gave it to me, is simple and like many simple dishes, delicious.

4 garlic cloves	1½ tablespoons chopped
3 tablespoons vegetable	parsley
or peanut oil	8 patty shells
6 green chili peppers	8 sprigs watercress
4 dozen small shrimp,	
cooked	

Preheat the oven to 450 degrees.

Peel and quarter garlic. Place oil in a small saucepan over low heat, add garlic and cook until it starts to brown. Remove and discard garlic. Meanwhile, cut off ends of chili peppers, and slice the peppers very thin, about ⅛ inch. Place them in the same saucepan, and cook slowly in the oil until they are soft. As peppers cook, dice the shrimp. Just before chili peppers are done, add the chopped shrimp and cook slowly, for about 1 minute. Remove pan from heat, stir contents, and, with a small slotted spoon, remove peppers and shrimp. Mix them with the chopped parsley and fill the shells with the mixture. Place filled shells in the preheated oven and bake until heated through. Garnish with a sprig of watercress each.

Beside each diner place a small individual bowl containing about 2 tablespoons of Penang Chili Sauce (page 165), that he may heighten the indigenous fire of the hors d'oeuvre if he likes.

Although they need not be served with the prawns, have available a few slices of pumpernickel or some pappadums against the needs of your guests who are not accustomed to fiery food. Water, beer, and wine are, in this case, paltry thirst quenchers.

Crab Apollyon

SERVES 6

If Apollyon had used this dish to delay Christian instead of fighting him for half a day, the Pilgrim's progress would have been much slowed if not brought to an abrupt halt. This crab will not lead you from the straight and narrow path if you are determined on it, but it could make you lose some of your determination to savor the flesh pots of Maryland. They compare not with those of Sodom and Gomorrah, but they exert enormous sensual influence.

This recipe is made from the backfin meat of the hard crab, and is served as a cold opening course.

To present Crab Apollyon properly you should have small individual ramekins, holding about 3 fluid ounces each.

4 rashers thick bacon	*½ teaspoon celery salt*
Butter	*2 teaspoons Worcester-*
1 pound backfin crab	*shire sauce*
lump	*¼ teaspoon Tabasco*
2 teaspoons prepared	*1 garlic clove, finely*
mustard	*minced*
¼ teaspoon cayenne	*3 tablespoons tartar sauce*

Preheat the oven to 300 degrees.

Cook bacon until crisp, and drain on paper towels. While bacon cooks, grease ramekins lightly but thoroughly with butter, and fill them with the crab. Place remaining ingredients in a small bowl and mix well at least twice. Cut the bacon small but do not mince. Sprinkle it over the top of the crab. Ten minutes before serving, place the ramekins in the preheated oven to heat through. Leave them for 3 minutes and remove. Mix contents of bowl again, and spread evenly over the top of each ramekin. Place the crabs under the broiler, grill, or in a salamander, and cook another 3 minutes. The crab should be served while it still bubbles.

Crab Apollyon is a fiery dish and should be so treated. Have thin slices of rye bread with caraway and a plate of butter on the table.

Lobster Lemonaid

SERVES 6

All marinades "cold cook" what is being marinated—be it meat, fowl, or as in this case, lobster. To be effective, however, the marinade must be able to work for hours. The acid of lemon juice acts slowly and its "cooking" time is prolonged. In this case you should allow a minimum of 12 hours; 24 is preferable. The cooking under a flame requires less than 10 minutes. You could start marination at 7 in the morning for dinner at 8 P.M., but 2 A.M. would be better. Best of all, start the night before.

The lobster should be cooked and served in large clam shells. So well before you start, get from your fishmonger 12 large, deep clam shells. However kindly disposed he is, the clam shells will demand additional cleaning. You must wash the shells first in hot water, and remove every vestige of clam with a knife and a wire brush. Then wash the clam shells in hot soapy water. Rinse in cold water and allow to dry. Troublesome, yes. But once done, the shells may be used many times for this hors d'oeuvre and other dishes.

2 frozen rock lobster tails
1 small onion
1 medium carrot
2 teaspoons minced
  parsley
2½ cups fresh lemon juice
1 bay leaf

Freshly ground black
  pepper
6 teaspoons Tabasco
Fine bread crumbs
Butter
12 sprigs watercress

Thaw lobster tails and remove meat in one piece from each shell. While lobster tails thaw, peel and chop the onion. Scrape carrot and cut into small dice. When lobster has thawed, place it in a shallow bowl large enough to hold the meat flat on the bottom. Cover with onion, carrot, parsley, and lemon juice. Add bay leaf. Place bowl in refrigerator. During the next 12, or however many hours you chose, turn lobster occasionally to keep meat covered with the marinade.

About 15 minutes before serving time, remove lobster from marinade. Cut meat into ½-inch cubes and fill the clam shells with the cubes. Pour a tablespoon of marinade over each serving, and sprinkle lightly with freshly ground black pepper. Add to each clam shell ½ teaspoon Tabasco. Sprinkle gently with bread crumbs and dot with butter. Put clam shells on a pan and place under a high broiler flame to brown crumbs, about 6 minutes. Garnish with watercress and serve while still hot.

Serve slices of buttered warm French bread with the lobster. A chilled white wine would be as welcome as the bread, but less effective as a fire extinguisher.

SOUPS

Most of the soups in this section are hearty and intended as the chief and, usually, only course for lunch or supper. It seems, however, meet to include preprandial thin broths and other soups which are ambidextrous and admit to being served either as the dish of the day, or, in lesser quantity, as the soup of the evening.

If there be virtue in the homeopathic theory that like cures like, these soups not only serve those who stand and wait at the buffet, but also those who have imbibed too much of the juice of the grape, barley, maize, rye, or potato. All those drinks are fiery, and if the theory is valid, the fire in the soups will counteract the fire in the drinks. This I cannot guarantee, but these soups will accelerate the flow of gastric juices and thus aid digestion.

You have here a baker's dozen of soups. That phrase dates from the days when a baker gave you thirteen rolls to a dozen. Today, alas, you are fortunate to find eleven rolls in the polyethylene package after you have torn finger nails, broken a tooth, or ruined the edge of your best paring knife trying to break through the impenetrable, impermeable, opaque shroud which now encloses, like armor plate, almost everything you buy. Rather a long digression, but good for the spleen. Back to our soups. I give you thirteen which will warm your throat, stomach, and the cockles of your heart. Make the most of them.

Chilied Beef Broth

SERVES 4

Here is one promised thin soup. It should be served hot; chilled it loses something of its fire. A hundred and more years ago most formal dinners began with two soups: one thin, the other thick. They were served simultaneously and the diner suited his fancy. Some, 'tis said, had both. Should you desire to emulate this custom and thus surprise many a guest, you could well use this broth and select as the second soup one of those heartier ones which follow.

Normally in consommé or bouillon julienne, the vegetables are sautéed in butter before being added to the broth. By using them raw and cooking only long enough in the broth to heat them, you get a crisper taste. To my palate, at least, this is highly rewarding. It also saves time in the kitchen. You can save more time by using two cans of condensed beef broth instead of making stock with bones and flesh.

10 or 12 fresh green chili peppers	*2¼ cups condensed beef broth*
1 small carrot	*¼ cup dry sherry*

Cut chili peppers into 1½-inch pieces. Split them and remove most but not all of the seeds, and all the membrane. Slice into julienne to make ½ cup. Scrape the carrot and cut into small dice, to make ¼ cup. Place the beef broth in a saucepan, add sherry, and vegetables. Cover and bring slowly to a simmer. Simmer covered, not more than 2 minutes and serve very hot.

This makes a medium fiery soup and you would be well advised to serve some kind of nonsalty wafers or crackers with it.

Gehennaise Soup

SERVES 4

After the conception of this book in Japan I crossed the broad Pacific by sea and pondered how the brainchild should be bred. Originally I had intended to devote the first section to fiery drinks. Empiricism clearly shows, however, that the only way to concoct a fiery drink is to use absolute alcohol, 151-proof rum, or to mix into a

Bloody Mary or its siblings an inadmissible quantity of Tabasco and Worcestershire sauce, and freshly ground black pepper. I dropped the drinks.

A cold soup made as below is a different, and, in the heat of the summer, a grateful starter to any meal. Even though cold it is fiery, and it is suitable as a soup course at luncheon or dinner. Unless you and your friends have internal sprinkler systems, do not serve the dish as the main course. Another peril of the soup is a tendency to inebriate. I doubt that you could become drunk from eating it, but follow the Boy Scouts and be prepared; you should also warn your guests. I suggest you do so by crying in stentorian tones: "caveat potor!" at the end of their first drink. Then proclaim that the soup contains vodka as a viable ingredient.

According to rabbinical theology, Gehenna is a place of eternal fire. On that basis alone the soup's qualifications for inclusion in this particular book are unimpeachable.

3 scallions	*¼ teaspoon Tabasco*
2 celery ribs	*¼ teaspoon freshly*
2¼ cups tomato juice	*ground black pepper*
1 tablespoon condensed	*1½ teaspoons lemon juice*
tomato soup	*¾ cup vodka*
1 teaspoon Worcester-	*Croutons*
shire sauce	

Chop scallions and celery into small pieces. Place other ingredients except croutons in a bowl, add scallions and celery. Mix well, and pour mixture into a blender. Blend at high speed for 10 seconds. Put in refrigerator for at least 1 hour, preferably 2. Return to blender and liquefy again for about 5 seconds. Serve in cream-soup plates with croutons on the side.

Gazpacho

SERVES 4

In culinary circles it is well known that there are as many ways of making paella as there are provinces in Spain. What is not so well known is that there are almost as many ways of making gazpacho as there are towns. That may be an exaggeration, but a slight one. This particular version comes from a town called Mojacar, situated on a

1500-foot hill, about two miles back from the Mediterranean. It is close to Almeria, which is near Cartagena, not far from Alicante. Now that you have pinpointed the location, a little history.

No one, including the mayor, who is also a physician and antiquarian, knows who built the original town. It could have been the Phoenicians, the Romans, the Moors, or the Spaniards themselves. Internal evidence leaves no doubt of Moorish influence. I first had this particular version of gazpacho at the home of a dear friend who has a triplex flat built into Mojacar's ancient walls. I reproduce the recipe here for three reasons. It is a fine dish; it is fiery; and it illustrates perfectly what I said in the introduction about hot versus fiery food.

1 large Spanish onion
2 large tomatoes
2 small cucumbers
1 large green bell pepper
4 garlic cloves
1 teaspoon freshly ground
  black pepper
1 teaspoon salt
1 teaspoon ground cumin
  seed

1 teaspoon dried basil or
  1 tablespoon minced
  fresh basil
2 tablespoons fresh lemon
  juice
¼ cup olive oil
2 cups tomato juice
4 dashes Tabasco
4 ice cubes
Croutons

Peel and chop the onion. Place in a large glass bowl. Skin the tomatoes and cucumbers; chop as small as the onion, and add to the bowl. Remove seeds and membranes from the green pepper and dice it. Put in bowl. Peel the garlic, put in a press or mince very fine, and distribute over the other vegetables. Add the freshly ground pepper, salt, cumin seed, basil, lemon juice, olive oil, tomato juice, 1 cup water, and Tabasco. Cover bowl and put in refrigerator for at least 3 hours. To serve: place an ice cube in each of 4 soup plates, fill plates with soup and serve croutons on the side.

Soup Senegalese

SERVES 4

This cold dish from Dakar is not so fiery as the streets of that city on a midsummer high noon, but it is sufficiently heating to warrant a place in this book and good enough to merit inclusion in any cookbook. The exact origin of the soup is uncertain, but its general sophistication and the use of curry powder indicates a strong French influence. The curry could have been brought to Senegal by French traders from the French holdings in India, and added as a spice to an indigenous West African recipe. Whatever its start, the soup is a splendid main dish for a lunch on a hot afternoon in Dakar or anywhere else.

Make the soup the day before you plan to serve it—it tastes better and is stronger after relaxing by itself in a refrigerator for 24 hours.

1 large onion	*1 tablespoon minced*
2 celery ribs	*fresh ginger*
1 large chicken breast,	*3 pints rich chicken stock*
cooked	*1 bay leaf*
1½ tablespoons butter	*¾ cup light cream*
1½ tablespoons sifted flour	*Salt*
2 tablespoons curry	*Pepper*
powder	

Chop the onion and the celery coarsely. Cut the chicken into fine dice, not larger than ¼ inch. Melt the butter in a saucepan, and cook the onion and celery until both are soft, but do not allow to brown. Add flour, curry powder, ginger, and make a smooth thick paste. Transfer contents of the saucepan to a blender. Add half the chicken —keep the other half in a cold place—and 1 cup of the chicken stock. Blend at high speed about 15 seconds. Return to saucepan, add remaining chicken stock and bay leaf. Bring to a boil, and simmer for 5 minutes. Remove and discard bay leaf. Transfer soup to a bowl and place in the refrigerator until needed. Just before serving, stir in the chilled cream, taste, and add salt and pepper as needed. Garnish with reserved diced chicken and serve forthwith.

Thrice Damned Pea Soup

SERVES 2 OR 4

Were this soup a pair of spectacles you might call it trifocal. It may be served, if you divide it into portions and make it hot, as a main luncheon or supper dish for two. You may serve it hot, in cream-soup cups as the opening course for a more elaborate meal for four; or, in summer, serve it cold in the same dishes for the same purpose.

If hot, serve croutons with it; if cold, top it with a dollop of sour cream. The recipe detailed below will make enough soup for any one of its three uses. Fiery it is but not too fiery.

As noted above it was once the custom at any formal dinner to serve two soups: one thin, the other thick. This pea soup and the chilied beef broth, previously described, would make an excellent combination to that end.

If your intent is to serve this soup hot, pour it directly from the blender into the top pan of a double boiler and warm over hot water. If it is to be a cold soup before dinner, pour from blender into a bowl and place in refrigerator to cool. When the soup is served cold, omit croutons. However you serve it, the soup is ridiculously easy to make.

1 pound fresh peas	*1 teaspoon fenugreek*
1 medium onion	* seeds*
1 small carrot	*2 cups chicken stock*
1 large celery rib with	*1 cup light cream*
* leaves*	*½ cup sour cream for*
1 large garlic clove	* serving soup cold*
1 teaspoon salt	* (optional)*
2 teaspoons curry powder	*Tabasco (optional)*

Shell the peas to make 1 cup. Peel onion and slice thinly. Scrape carrot, and cut into thin slices. Chop the celery, including the leaves, into moderately coarse pieces. Mash or mince the garlic. Place the peas, onions, carrot, garlic, salt, curry powder, and fenugreek seeds into a saucepan and add 1 cup of stock. Cover, bring to a boil, and reduce heat to simmer. Simmer 18 minutes. Remove from heat and allow to cool for 5 minutes. Pour mixture into a blender, blend briefly, and gradually add remaining stock and the cream. Blend another 5 seconds and the dish is done. Serve hot or chilled as above. (If back taste is not fiery enough stir in 1 teaspoon Tabasco.)

Gingered Chicken Soup

SERVES 6

For reasons beyond my ken, this is known in some quarters as curried soup although it contains no curry powder. Hence it would seem more Chinese than Indian. Aside from its unquestionable excellence and its fire, the soup has another merit: it may be served two ways. By including cut-up chicken you have a hearty main dish for lunch or a late supper. Omit the chicken and you have a kind of pseudo-Chinese broth suitable as a soup course. Use it when you like, but remember you should allow considerable time for preparation. Best make it one day and serve the next, adding the watercress at the last moment. Gingered Chicken Soup is neither easy nor fast —but is well worth the time and trouble.

2 large onions
4 thick scallions
1 piece fresh ginger, 1 inch long by 1½ inches wide and ¾ inch thick
1 lemon
1 four-pound chicken
3 tablespoons kosher salt
12 black peppercorns
1 bay leaf
2 teaspoons fenugreek seeds

1½ cups bean sprouts, drained
2 parsley sprigs
½ bunch watercress
1 tablespoon vegetable oil
1 tablespoon ground ginger
Salt
Freshly ground white pepper

Peel and chop onions. Slice scallions, including part of green tops. Peel and chop ginger into small pieces. Quarter lemon. Rub the chicken inside and out with 2 pieces of lemon and put chicken into a soup kettle or large stock pot. Add half the chopped onion, the scallions, the fresh ginger, remaining lemon, salt, peppercorns, bay leaf, and fenugreek. Pour 5 pints water into pot. Cover pot and simmer 2½ hours. Remove chicken and allow to cool. Strain stock and retain. Discard contents of strainer. Place stock in refrigerator. While chicken cools, drain bean sprouts; mince parsley, and chop watercress, retaining some of the tender stems.

When chicken is cool enough to handle pick meat from bones, discarding the latter and any skin, gristle, or fat. Chop meat into very small chunks. Refrigerate. Place oil in a heavy iron skillet over low heat. When oil is hot add remaining chopped onion. Cook slowly until soft. Add ground ginger. Stir and allow to bubble 2 or 3 minutes. Meanwhile remove stock from refrigerator, skim off the fat, and pour stock into the soup pot or saucepan. Bring to a boil. Reduce to simmer and add contents of skillet along with chopped chicken, bean sprouts, and parsley. Cover and simmer another 10 minutes. Put in watercress, and, stirring continuously, simmer another 2 or 3 minutes. Season to taste with salt and white pepper. Serve immediately.

If you serve the soup as a main course, you should have some kind of mild salad—perhaps a bowl of torn lettuce and a French dressing. The soup is not so fiery as to *demand* bread, but a light rye would not be amiss. The driest of Graves, well chilled, would be a happy wine selection.

Pakistani Tiger Soup

SERVES 2 OR 4

Home is the hunter, home from the hills and with an empty bag. When that happens in Wales, the hunter is rewarded by his helpmate for his efforts however unavailing. She gives him Welsh rabbit, a concoction of cheese and beer. In Pakistan, the hunter, after listening to a few well-chosen words about his ancestry, is fed tiger soup. This fiery broth is double-first cousin to the mulligatawny made in Ceylon. The tiger in the title is intended to be ironic as is the rabbit in Welsh rabbit. Any similarity between the Welsh reward and that of Pakistan is not merely coincidental; it is ridiculous.

Tiger soup serves two masters. Unlike a servant, it serves each equally well. It may be used as the main dish for a lunch or supper. Thus it is given to the unlucky hunter. Or the dish may be served as a soup course before dinner. If this is your choice, I suggest that it be garnished with a sprinkling of finely chopped fresh chives. The recipe will make enough soup for two for a main course, and for four if served in bouillon cups.

The recipe for the condiment paste will be enough for twice the amount of soup as described below. Put the unused paste in a small, tightly covered jar and refrigerate. It will last for at least a week.

½ teaspoon ground
  cinnamon
½ teaspoon curry powder
1 teaspoon cracked black
  pepper
¼ teaspoon fenugreek
  seeds
2 teaspoons minced
  garlic
½ teaspoon dry mustard
½ teaspoon ground ginger
1 teaspoon ground cumin
  seed
¼ teaspoon whole cumin
  seed

1 tablespoon ground
  coriander
½ teaspoon mustard seed
1 tablespoon chopped
  dried red chili pepper
3½ cups beef or chicken
  stock
1 medium onion
½ tablespoon butter
1 tomato
1 cup cubed lean cooked
  lamb or chicken
½ cup milk

Mix first 12 ingredients thoroughly in a bowl. Add ½ cup of stock (chicken stock if using cooked chicken) and mix again. Place in a blender. Blend at high speed for about 1 minute. Remove from blender and return to bowl. This is the paste.

Peel and chop onion. Melt butter in a heavy 2-quart saucepan, add onion, and cook, stirring now and then, until onion is translucent. Meanwhile peel tomato and chop coarsely. Add to saucepan and continue to cook over low heat. Place 2 generous teaspoons of seasoning paste on top of onions and tomatoes. Add cubed lamb or chicken. Pour in the remaining stock. Cover, bring to a boil, reduce heat, and simmer for about 25 minutes. Add milk and pour contents of saucepan into blender. Mix at medium speed for about 90 seconds.

If you plan to serve immediately, return to saucepan and bring just to a simmer. Serve at once. If you want to serve the soup later, transfer from blender to a bowl and refrigerate until about 30 minutes before reheating.

If used as a main dish, or even as a soup before dinner, I suggest you provide your guests with black bread, with or without butter. Probably the best wine with the soup at lunch or supper would be a well-chilled, red Tavola from California. And by all means a green salad, or at each plate half a ripe avocado with salt and pepper.

Pepit's Shrimp Potage

SERVES 4

One of Pepit's favorite luncheon dishes is a hot and fiery shrimp soup. He believes that the alcoholic poison he imbibes every morning, under medicinal guise, is best offset at lunch by a relatively heavy soup. Like most of Pepit's recipes, its origin is obscure. He spends much time with an aunt in Italy, and I suspect he learned about this dish from that amiable lady. Wherever he got it, the soup merits your attention.

With it he invariably drinks chilled white Machiavelli Chianti. I can think of no better combination. Small side dishes of croutons would be a welcome addition.

4 cups peeled and chopped ripe tomatoes or 1 one-pound-twelve-ounce can Italian plum tomatoes	Salt
	1 teaspoon curry powder
	1 teaspoon chili powder
	¼ teaspoon ground ginger
	¼ teaspoon ground allspice
3 celery ribs	½ teaspoon cayenne
6 scallions	½ cup dry sherry
3 tablespoons chopped parsley	1 pound cooked tiny shrimp
1 bay leaf	½ cup milk
1 teaspoon white pepper	

Place the tomatoes in a large saucepan over medium heat. Chop the celery and scallions, including the green tops. Add these and the parsley to the tomatoes along with bay leaf, ½ cup water, white pepper, and salt to taste. Bring to a boil and simmer 20 minutes.

Meanwhile mix the curry and chili powders, the ginger, allspice, and cayenne in a second, smaller saucepan; add sherry and bring to a boil. Reduce heat and put in the shrimp. Cover and heat for not more than 3 minutes.

When the basic tomato stock has cooked, put it through a food mill, return to the first saucepan, and place it over a low flame. Add contents of second saucepan and gradually pour in the milk, stirring as you pour. Taste and season with salt and pepper if needed. Simmer gently for 5 minutes and serve.

Mulligatawny

SERVES 6

Not an especially esoteric soup, mulligatawny is well known all over the world. The Singhalese dish is made in various ways, each of which produces a fiery dish. The fire depends on the amount of curry powder and cayenne you use. The soup can be comparatively mild, but this recipe from Ceylon is not for the mealy mouthed, or for those whose digestion is fragile.

An etymological culinary note might be both edifying and amusing. Mulligatawny is a Tamil word which, literally translated, means "pepper water." And so it is. But I have been somewhat astonished at the number of people who think the soup originated in Ireland. Doubtless they were thinking of mulligan stew, which is not Irish either. Rather it is an American dish, probably invented by tramps, in which everything they can find—rabbit, squirrel, chicken, carrots, onions, potatoes—is combined in a pot with water to make a thick, wholesome dish if it is simmered long enough. Later or perhaps earlier, it was a "camp stew" used by hunting parties to make a kind of slumgullion. Mulligatawny soup is neither a stew nor is it Irish.

2½ pounds cooked lamb	2 tablespoons curry
2 medium onions	powder
2 tart medium apples	4 tablespoons sifted flour
1 medium turnip	1½ teaspoons cayenne
1 ten-ounce can baby	3 ten-ounce cans beef
carrots	broth
1 tablespoon bacon fat	1 quart chicken stock
3 tablespoons butter	1 cup cooked rice

Remove and discard all fat and gristle from meat and cut it into ½-inch cubes. Peel onions, apples, and turnip. Drain carrots. Chop all into medium dice. Heat bacon fat and butter in a large saucepan. Add diced onions and turnip, and cook over slow fire for about 10 minutes, stirring occasionally. While vegetables cook, mix curry powder, flour, and cayenne well in a small bowl. Add apples and carrots to saucepan, and cook another 5 minutes. Blend in the curry mixture and cook an additional 5 minutes, stirring to prevent scorching. Meanwhile, combine the beef broth and chicken stock and bring to a boil. Remove from heat. Add the hot mixed stock a little at a time to the contents of the saucepan, stirring constantly to prevent lumping, and make a smooth, slightly thick soup. Put in the meat cubes, stir well, and bring to a boil. Allow to simmer boldly, still stirring, for about 2 minutes. Reduce heat, cover, and simmer soup gently for 30 minutes. Add rice and serve.

Mustard Soup Tisel

SERVES 4

Adages rule my life. It is easier to quote them than to invent new ones. One of the adages is: "There is nothing new under the sun." The aphorism applies in many fields, but nowhere more than in cookery. Some years ago I found a gadget which poked a tiny hole in the butt of an egg so that you could plunge an almost frigid egg directly into boiling water without fear of its splitting. I thought the gadget was a product of American ingenuity and know-how. Accidental research while I lay on a bed of pain recovering from Hong Kong flu revealed that the needling of an egg had been discovered midway in the fourteenth century.

At about the same time that the egg-needler made his discovery, another cook, Guillaume Tisel, created a luscious mustard soup. Tisel, known as Taillevent, was chef to French royalty. The soup may be served either hot or cold, but will always be fiery. You can, therefore, put it together a day or two before you plan to use it and serve either out of the refrigerator or reheat it in a double boiler. If served hot, garnish with two dozen paper-thin slices of peperoni.

With the soup I suggest a very tart white wine, and medium slices of black bread.

3 tablespoons butter	*3 egg yolks*
3 tablespoons flour	*4 tablespoons heavy*
3½ cups hot chicken stock	*cream*
2½ cups milk	*5 tablespoons hot*
½ teaspoon salt	*prepared mustard*
½ teaspoon white pepper	*24 slices peperoni*
1 tablespoon grated	*(optional)*
onion	

Melt the butter and stir in the flour. Blend smooth. Add the hot chicken stock and milk, and whisk until smooth. Add salt, pepper, and grated onion. Simmer for 10 to 15 minutes. Cool slightly. Combine egg yolks and cream and add to the soup, custard style—that is, temper eggs first with a few spoonfuls of the warm broth. Add the mustard last, and mix it well into the soup before serving.

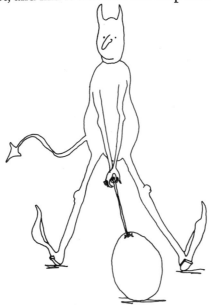

Philadelphia Pepper Pot

SERVES 4

This famous Pennsylvania soup is made with tripe and time—it takes over two days. Tripe is the lining of a cow's stomach. Legend has it that the dish was invented by a cook in the Continental Army during the terrible winter at Valley Forge and that the soup saved the Revolution. I don't believe it. No army cook, except possibly one attached to Lafayette's own mess, ever had the imagination or skill to create so succulent a dish.

The soup takes two days or approximately eighteen hours to make. For much of that time, however, it may be left unattended. Once the two pots have begun to simmer they need scant watching for five hours. Later, both broths must be refrigerated overnight or for at least eight hours. Actual time in the kitchen amounts to three hours; even that can be reduced by speedy preparation. Ask your butcher to provide a cracked marrow bone with plenty of marrow in it. The marrow may be removed with the bowl or handle of a spoon or with a dull knife, depending on the shape of the space to be emptied.

All recipes should be read through at least once before being attempted for the first time. This recipe should be read at least twice. The soup is well worth the effort and it will keep, refrigerated, for several days. The dumplings, however, must be made fresh.

First Day

1 pound tripe	tied together in
1 medium onion	cheesecloth)
1 medium carrot	1 teaspoon cracked red
1 small marrow bone	pepper
1 veal knuckle	1¼ teaspoons ground
Bouquet garni (1 bay leaf,	allspice
2 sprigs parsley, ½	· 4 cloves
teaspoon dry mustard	

Wash tripe well, put in soup kettle, add 5 quarts water. Bring to a boil, reduce heat and simmer, covered, 7 hours. Peel and slice onion and carrot. Remove marrow from bone, and place in a skillet. Melt marrow, put in onion and carrot slices and cook over moderate heat, stirring occasionally, until onion is soft. Meanwhile, put veal knuckle into another soup kettle or large saucepan; cover with 5 quarts water. Put the marrow bone in with the veal knuckle, add contents of skillet, the bouquet garni, cracked red pepper, allspice, and cloves. Bring to a boil, cover, and simmer 5 hours. When veal knuckle has finished cooking, remove pot from fire and allow to cool. When veal can be comfortably handled, remove and dice any edible meat; reserve. Discard all bones. Discard bouquet garni. Strain broth; place in a mixing bowl, cover, and refrigerate.

When tripe is done, remove kettle from fire and set aside until meat is cool enough to handle. Dice it. Place broth, covered, in refrigerator. Mix chopped tripe and veal, if any, and stow in refrigerator. All 3 bowls should remain in refrigerator overnight or at least 8 hours.

Second Day

2 medium potatoes	⅛ teaspoon salt
1 teaspoon marjoram	1½ teaspoons shortening
2 teaspoons salt	4 tablespoons milk
2 teaspoons freshly	2 tablespoons minced
ground black pepper	parsley
½ cup flour	4 tablespoons dry sherry
1 teaspoon baking	
powder	

Remove bowls from refrigerator. Skim and discard fat from both broths. Combine broths in a large soup kettle. Peel and dice the potatoes and add to kettle. Put in the tripe and veal, the marjoram, salt, and pepper. Bring to a boil, and simmer, covered, 45 minutes.

Combine flour, baking powder, and salt. Sift them into a bowl, add shortening and cut in or mix well with fingers. After soup has simmered for 45 minutes, add milk to flour mixture and stir well with a fork to make a dough for dumplings. Bring soup to a rapid boil and put in dumpling dough, a half teaspoon at a time. Add minced parsley and sherry. Reduce heat, and simmer, covered, for 15 minutes. The soup is now ready to serve.

Bread will neither be needed nor missed. A salad of cooked beets, endive, and sliced cucumber with vinaigrette sauce is good with this soup. A good, full-bodied red wine would enhance the meal.

Dahl

SERVES 4

The recipe for this soup was given me by a physical anthropologist lent by Harvard to the Thai Government to make some studies of the northern tribes. In the town where he made his headquarters there was, in addition to a motion picture palace, a small restaurant which made a specialty of lentil soup. The proprietor would bring out steaming bowls to my friend and his wife that they might eat in their car. They always stopped by for a bowl of dahl, as he called the soup, each time they went to the movies, which was often. The town suffered from a paucity of entertainment.

This meatless soup is an extremely useful lunch or supper dish for guests who are observing Lent or for others who may be vegetarians by conviction rather than faith. One of the great advantages of this soup is that even for carnivorous animals such as I, it makes excellent eating; it can be served with complete assurance to any company.

With skill and attention, dahl may be cooked in an hour. With very little skill, the soup can be prepared readily in 75 minutes. The finished product should be on the thick side, about the consistency of a full-bodied Dutch pea soup. If thinning is required, use water. The recipe calls for quick-cooking lentils.

1 cup quick-cooking lentils	*4 tablespoons curry powder*
Salt	*2 tablespoons ground*
2 tablespoons turmeric	*allspice*
2 medium onions	*1 garlic clove*
1 medium green bell	*1 teaspoon lemon juice*
pepper	*Bombay duck (optional)*
4 tablespoons butter	

Wash the lentils until the water is clear. Place them in a large saucepan. Add 3 pints water, 1 teaspoon salt, and the turmeric.

Bring to a boil. Cover, and simmer for 50 minutes. Chop onions and green pepper coarsely. Melt butter in a skillet. Add the onions, green pepper, curry powder, and allspice. Mince the garlic fine or put it through a press and add to the skillet. Cook over moderate heat, stirring frequently, until the onion is lightly brown. Add lemon juice and cook 5 minutes longer. Add contents of the skillet to the saucepan. Stir well, taste. Add salt as required.

If you use the Bombay duck, crisp it before you start on the soup so that it may cool. It is used for garnish, as well as for flavor. Allow 2 pieces of the little dried fish for each diner. Place the fish in a preheated 450-degree oven and brown until the edges begin to curl. Remove from oven to a cool place but do not refrigerate. Pappadums or brown bread should be served with the soup.

Mangrove Bay Fish Chowder

SERVES 4 OR 6

Fish chowder is not one of my favorites. A seafaring friend produced a bowl of the soup after a recent incursion into Bermuda waters. I found it delicious and fiery enough to become the thirteenth dish in this section and thus complete the baker's dozen. If even as I, you find fish chowder less than attractive, give this one a whirl. Perhaps I should stress that I am using fish rather than seafood. Seafood chowders are an entirely different kettle of fish.

The original recipe comes from the Gamefish Inn in Somerset. It calls for wahoo, a fish found off Bermuda, Florida, and in the West Indies. For the test recipe I used striped bass. Any fish with firm white flesh will do. Ask your fishmonger to scale, skin, and fillet the fish. One essential, however, is that you bring the heads and bones home for making a fumet. Another essential is that you use curry paste and not curry powder. The difference is marked in taste, texture, and appearance.

The following quantity of chowder will make a filling meal for four people; it will also serve six or eight as a first course.

Butter	*2 tablespoons curry paste*
2 large onions	*½ tablespoon dried*
10 parsley stalks	*thyme*
1½ pounds fish heads and	*1 bay leaf*
bones	*¼ cup Worcestershire*
2 tablespoons lemon	*sauce*
juice	*¼ cup tomato ketchup*
1 cup dry white wine	*1 pound fish fillets,*
½ cup chopped celery	*skinned*
½ pound thickly sliced	*Salt*
lean bacon	*Pepper*

First make a fumet by combining in a large saucepan the butter, 1 onion, parsley stalks, fish heads and bones, lemon juice, wine, and 2½ quarts cold water. Simmer for about 30 minutes.

While fumet simmers, peel and chop other onion coarsely. Place in a bowl with the celery and set aside. Cut bacon rashers in half and sauté them lightly in a skillet, until done but not crisp. Drain on paper towels. Leave 2 tablespoons of bacon fat in skillet, discarding remainder. Place the chopped onion, and celery in skillet and cook over low heat, stirring to prevent burning, until onion and celery are soft. Meanwhile cut cooked bacon into squares. When onion and celery are soft, put curry paste in skillet, and combine well. Cook, stirring constantly, for about 3 minutes.

Allow fumet to cool, then strain and discard fish bones and vegetables. Return fumet to heat and add contents of skillet, the bacon squares, the thyme, bay leaf, Worcestershire sauce, and ketchup. Cut fish fillets into 1½-inch pieces and toss them into the saucepan. Cover, bring to a boil, reduce heat, and simmer for 15 minutes. Uncover saucepan, remove and discard bay leaf. Taste and correct seasoning with salt and pepper as required. With the cover off the saucepan, continue to simmer very slowly for another 15 minutes, stirring with a wooden spoon occasionally. The chowder is now ready and should be served very hot.

You should offer some kind of bread with the soup. I used homemade bread seasoned with parmesan cheese and oregano. Rye bread seasoned with caraway seeds is another possibility. If the chowder is to be a main dish serve with it a salad of sliced peeled tomatoes and sliced green peppers on a lettuce leaf. As for wine, you have two choices: a very dry Spanish sherry or a very dry chilled white wine.

EGGS AND PASTA

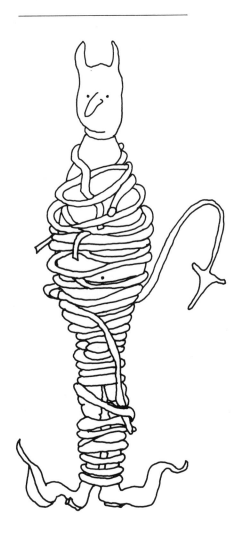

Why put eggs and pasta in the same section? The truth is that I did not have enough fiery recipes for either to warrant a section for each. Then, too, you cannot make pasta without breaking eggs. Besides being a reason for combining the two types of dishes, it is a plea to you to make your own pasta.

Most kinds of pasta, from vermicelli to cannelloni, are available in Italian grocery stores and even in supermarkets. Most of the brands, especially those sold in the chain stores are related in name only to their Italian counterparts. A few of the Italian imports are good; your friendly Italian grocer can advise you. In no case, however, will the pasta you buy be so good as the pasta you make, if only because you can control the egg content, a most important ingredient. Your initial efforts may seem arduous and messy, but after a little practice the process will become easier, and the results most rewarding.

To make pasta at home requires a pasta machine, a small, comparatively inexpensive device which rolls the dough to the desired thickness and then cuts it into various widths depending on the type of pasta you want, be it anything from vermicelli to lasagne.

Eggs

Dairyman's Eggs

SERVES 8

This homely way of preparing highly seasoned eggs is aptly named, calling as it does for butter, cheese, eggs, sour cream, and light cream. It is absurdly easy and is highly recommended for an informal lunch or supper if you have unexpected guests. Most, if not all, of the ingredients you will already have in your larder or refrigerator. The dish can be prepared and cooked in about 30 minutes.

Butter	*1 teaspoon salt*
½ pound sharp cheddar	*1 cup sour cream*
cheese, shredded	*4 tablespoons light cream*
16 eggs	*4 tablespoons minced*
5 teaspoons dry mustard	*parsley*
1 teaspoon cayenne	

Preheat the oven to 350 degrees.

Lightly grease 8 ramekins with butter and line each with cheese. Break 2 eggs into each ramekin—you can make small indentations in the cheese for the eggs if it seems they might overflow. Mix the spices together, then mix the sour cream with the light cream. Gradually stir the cream mixture into the spice mix until smooth. Pour over the eggs and dot with butter. Bake for 15 minutes. Just before serving, garnish with the minced parsley.

A small salad, and buttered, hot melba toast are good with the eggs. Dry white wine or champagne, of course.

Ham and Eggs en Cocotte

SERVES 4

Most ham and egg combinations make for insipid, mundane breakfast dishes. Not so this combination for some meal after noon. It smacks of fire and brimstone but has no sulphuric taste. The recipe is said to come from Tunis. I doubt it. Moslems are not overly partial to ham in any form. Regardless of its origin, the dish will warm the throat and the stomach.

4 medium onions	*3 large thin green chili*
3 garlic cloves	*peppers*
3 tablespoons butter	*2 medium slices baked*
2 large green bell peppers	*ham, ¼ inch thick*
2 small, firm tomatoes	*8 large eggs*

Peel onions and chop coarsely. Mash garlic. Melt butter in a large skillet, add onions and garlic, and cook over medium heat, stirring now and again, until onions are almost transparent. Meanwhile remove membranes and seeds from the bell peppers, and chop them coarsely. Add to skillet. Maneuver contents with a large spoon until vegetables are well coated with butter and juices. Skin tomatoes and chop coarsely. Remove heads and tails of the chili peppers but do not remove seeds. Cut into pieces about ¼-inch long. Put tomatoes and hot peppers into skillet and stir them in well. Continue cooking until vegetables are almost reduced to a pulp.

Preheat the oven to 350 degrees.

Dice ham, removing and discarding all fat. Divide the vegetable mixture among 4 cocottes or gratin dishes. Sprinkle the diced ham on top of the vegetables. Break 2 eggs into each cocotte. Place the cocottes in the oven and bake for 15 minutes. If you like runny eggs reduce the time to about 10 minutes.

Plain buttered toast, hot hard rolls, or popovers, according to your fancy, go well with these eggs.

Eggs in a Pet

SERVES 4

These pettish eggs were invented by a man in a pet and furious at himself for being in a pet and at the people who put him there. The pet lasted only long enough for him to devise the recipe and cook it. He got a good scrambled-egg dish out of his fury. His temporary loss of temper is your permanent gastronomic gain.

4 green chili peppers	*2 teaspoons dry mustard*
10 eggs	*¼ teaspoon salt*
1½ tablespoons minced	*1½ tablespoons butter*
chives	*Cayenne*

Sliver the chili peppers lengthwise and remove all the membranes and most of the seeds. Mince. Break the eggs into a bowl. Add chili peppers, chives, dry mustard, and salt. Melt butter in a large heavy skillet, coating bottom and sides. Beat the egg mixture until it is completely melded. Pour into skillet and cook, stirring to scramble the eggs thoroughly. When done, powder lightly with cayenne and serve on hot plates forthwith. It is well to have the guests at the table just before the eggs are ready.

Hot crusty buttered rolls, and a green salad with cut up avocado and a simple French dressing would take a little fire from the eggs and make them more palatable for some. Cold beer is an appropriate accompanying drink.

Eggs Simla

SERVES 4

I am indebted for this recipe to my old friend and redoubtable trencherman, the late Brigadier Smithson Browne-Jones, D.S.O., M.C., O.B.E., of the Anglo-Indian Army. During the time of the Raj, and when he was not with troops, the brigadier would spend the hot months with friends in Simla. He told me that he found the dish excellent as a late breakfast or at tiffin. It was not, he said, a good campaign diet; for that you should have mutton.

8 eggs	*2 teaspoons ground ginger*
6 rashers bacon	*2 tablespoons butter*
2 tablespoons flour	*1 cup chicken stock*
1 teaspoon curry powder	*½ cup milk*
2 teaspoons dry mustard	*Paprika*

Hard cook the eggs—boil about 10 minutes. Fry the bacon until crisp and chop into ½-inch squares. Keep warm. Meanwhile place flour, curry powder, dry mustard, and ground ginger in a bowl and mix them well. Melt butter in a saucepan over low flame. Heat stock and milk in a separate saucepan. When butter has melted, add flour mixture and make a paste, stirring constantly for about 2 minutes. Gradually add stock and milk, to make a sauce. Stir from time to time to keep from scorching. During this interval, shell eggs and halve them lengthwise. When sauce has come to a boil, it is done. It should be medium thick. If too thick, thin with additional chicken stock.

Place the eggs, cut side down, on a hot platter. Sprinkle with bacon squares, and pour sauce over them. Garnish lightly with paprika and serve at once.

Eggs Simla are not so fiery that they need an extinguisher, but a sliced, skinned tomato on a bit of lettuce, seasoned with a little dill and a sprinkle of salt would be welcome. Put a small toast round under each egg half. Ale is preferred to wine as a potable.

Celery Soufflé

SERVES 4

Among my wife's contributions to the recipes is this moderately fiery soufflé. In addition to soufflés, to which she brings exactly the right feminine touch needed by so delicate a dish, she is also the popover and crêpe cook as well as the waffleteer—a lovely word. On a day when I was in the middle of writing up a recipe, Mrs. C. prepared a cheese soufflé for lunch. Afterwards I naturally praised her efforts and said it would be a good thing were there a fiery soufflé. She allowed as how she'd try her hand at it. She did. The result was worthy, if not scorching. Should you want more fire, increase the cayenne but not the cardamom.

1 cup coarsely chopped
celery
¼ pound sharp cheese
4 eggs
4 tablespoons butter
4 tablespoons flour
1⅓ cups milk
½ teaspoon cayenne

1 teaspoon ground
cardamom
½ teaspoon salt
1 teaspoon Worcester-
shire sauce
4 dashes Tabasco
Paprika

Simmer the celery, covered, in lightly salted boiling water for 6 minutes. Grate cheese. Separate eggs. Melt butter in a large skillet, add flour and stir to make a roux, but do not let it brown. Warm the milk and add to roux to make a white sauce. When smooth and simmering, reduce heat, and add cheese, stirring steadfastly. Drain celery, add to skillet, along with cayenne, cardamom, salt, Worcestershire, and Tabasco. Stir in thoroughly. Lightly beat the egg yolks and add to the sauce. Allow the mixture to cool for at least 20 minutes.

Preheat oven to 350 degrees. Beat egg whites until stiff and dry, and fold into cheese-celery mixture. Pour contents of skillet into a 7-inch soufflé dish, sprinkle liberally with paprika and bake in oven for 40 minutes or until brown on top.

Baby artichoke hearts with Mustard Dressing (p. 156) supplies a salad and a vegetable. A white wine, of course.

Ham Soufflé

SERVES 4

You can't have too much of a good thing. When the preceding soufflé proved such a flaming success, I suggested that another one made with the classic combination of ham and mustard might not come amiss. My good wife produced with her expert touch this delicious and even more fiery ham soufflé.

2 slices baked ham,	*5 tablespoons sifted flour*
¼ inch thick	*1⅔ cups milk*
4 tablespoons Bavarian	*¼ cup grated parmesan*
mustard	*cheese*
4 tablespoons Moselle	*5 eggs*
wine	*¾ teaspoon Tabasco*
5 tablespoons butter	*¼ teaspoon cayenne*

About 2 hours before you are ready to cook the soufflé, grind ham finely. Place in a small bowl. Mix the mustard and wine. Pour over ham and integrate thoroughly. Set aside and let stand for at least 1 hour. Melt butter in a skillet, add flour and stir until smooth, then cook about 2 minutes. Gradually add milk stirring the while until contents of skillet begin to boil. When sauce is smooth, stir in cheese, reduce heat. Add ham and mustard mixture and mix well. Meanwhile separate eggs. Beat the yolks lightly and stir into the mixture in the skillet. Cook over low heat for a minute or two and add Tabasco and cayenne. Remove from heat and allow to stand idly by to cool for a minimum of 15 minutes, 20 would be better.

Preheat the oven to 350 degrees.

Beat the egg whites stiff and fold into the mixture in the skillet. Pour contents of skillet into an ungreased 2-quart soufflé dish, and place in the preheated oven for 50 minutes. Under no circumstances —let the house burn down first—open the oven door. Remove soufflé from oven and serve at once.

Buttered toast would be a good starchy accompaniment with the soufflé. You will require, I think, a salad. Why not a bed of Bibb lettuce, covered by fresh avocado chunks and a vinaigrette sauce? Why not indeed? The wine can be either red or white.

Catalan Tortilla

SERVES 4

In Mexico a tortilla is a flat round kind of bread made from maize; in Spain a tortilla is an omelet. Not a plain omelet, but one filled with vegetables, offal, or a combination thereof. The tortilla has no resemblance to the Spanish omelet beloved of minor lunch rooms and other eateries in the United States. The stuffings of Granada, Seville, Valencia, Cordoba, to name a few, all differ. Basically they are made the same way. You prepare the filling and cook it in a modicum of oil in a heavy iron skillet. Then mix it with the eggs.

For the most part tortillas are bland, but, the good tortilla cook will always add a bit of fiery seasoning to his dish. This particular tortilla has more fire than the average.

1 large tomato	3 tablespoons vegetable
1 large onion	oil
1 large celery rib	10 eggs
2 chorizos (sausages)	1 teaspoon salt
6 small dried red chili	1 teaspoon freshly ground
peppers	black pepper

Skin tomato and onion. Chop them and celery coarsely. Coarsely chop the chorizos. Cut the chili peppers small. Put half the oil in a large heavy iron skillet and heat over a moderate flame. When oil is hot, swirl pan gently so that at least 1 inch of the sides is coated. Put in chopped vegetables and chorizos. Stirring from time to time, coat them with oil; cook until they are soft but not mushy. Meanwhile place eggs in a large mixing bowl, add salt and pepper, and beat well until the color and consistency are uniform. When contents of skillet are done, and this is important, pour mixture into beaten eggs. *Never* vice versa. Be sure the skillet contains no residue of its contents. Return to stove, and raise heat. When skillet is thoroughly hot, pour mixture from bowl into skillet and allow to cook, without altering heat, until sides of the mixture are brown.

Now things get a bit tricky. Don a pair of heatproof gloves. Place a flat close-fitting lid with a handle over the skillet and invert it so that the half-cooked tortilla comes out and lies flat on the lid. Holding that in your left hand, add remaining oil to skillet. Coat the pan again, and when oil is hot, slide the tortilla off the lid into the skillet. If done precisely the whole tortilla will slip into the skillet and what had been the uncooked top will become the bottom. Allow to cook until the bottom is brown. Serve at once. This sounds complex; it *is* the first time you try. Experience will make the process quicker and easier. Persevere. If at first . . . and all that sort of thing.

Spanish bread, if you can get it, or French bread is appropriate with the tortilla. The wine should be Spanish. If that be unavailable, I suggest a white or red Tavola from California. Be sure it is well chilled, regardless of color.

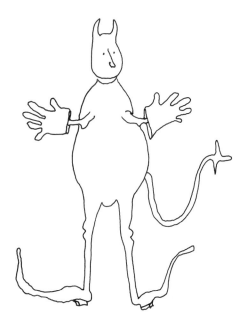

Scotch Eggs

SERVES 4

To say that Scots live on porridge, haggis, grouse, and whiskey is a base canard. They also eat, among other things: eggs and sausage; duck, another canard; and dunlop cheese. Scotch eggs are not to be confused with such dishes as Scotch woodcock, which is neither Scotch nor bird; or with Welsh rabbit which is Welsh but contains no rabbit. Scotch eggs are made with eggs and a highly flavored sausage made from the meat of Scotch pigs.

Scotch eggs are both cold *and* fiery. The trouble and mess of deep frying is commensurate with the result. The sausage seasoning adds some kindling to the fire, but the real fire derives from the sauce, which tastes as though it had been brought straight from Hell. The eggs will have to cool in the refrigerator for at least eight hours so you may make the sauce when you like. It will keep unrefrigerated at least 24 hours.

Sauce

2 cups mayonnaise
4 tablespoons prepared
   hot horseradish
1 tablespoon lemon juice

2 teaspoons ground
   cardamom
½ teaspoon cayenne

Mix all together well in a bowl and chill until ready for use. Mix sauce fervently again just before serving it.

The Eggs and Sausage

3 cups vegetable oil
8 day-old eggs
2 pounds bulk spiced
   sausage meat

2 fresh eggs
1 cup bread crumbs

Place oil in saucepan over low heat. Bring gradually to 375 degrees for deep frying. Meanwhile, place day-old eggs in a saucepan of hot water, bring to a boil, and cook long enough to harden the eggs that they may be shelled, about 10 minutes. Drain eggs, and run cold water over them until they are chilled. Refrigerate. While eggs cool place sausage on a bread board and form it into a thin layer about a ¼ inch thick. Shell eggs. Using your hands, completely cover each egg evenly with the sausage to make a kind of cocoon. Break fresh eggs into a bowl and beat them well. With a pastry brush paint each sausaged egg with a light coat of the beaten eggs. Spread bread crumbs on a counter and roll the eggs in the crumbs to cover them.

The oil should now be hot. Unless you have a very large deep fryer, do 2 eggs at a time. They must cool before use in any case. Place 2 prepared eggs into your deep-fry basket and leave them in the fat until brown on the outside. What you seek is a crusty coating on the outside, a cooked but soft sausage second layer, and a hard-cooked but nonleathery egg in the middle. Depending on the type of fat you use and the temperature—the coated eggs should cook 5 to 6 minutes—you may require two or three attempts to get exactly the result you want.

When the first eggs are cooked, remove and drain on paper towels. Bring the fat back to 375 degrees and repeat above process with the 6 remaining eggs. Now place eggs in refrigerator overnight or for a minimum of 8 hours.

Serving

1 large head of Bibb lettuce   *2 tomatoes*

About 1 hour before serving, shred lettuce and wrap in a dish towel until needed. Skin tomatoes and cut each into 4 slices. Make a bed of the lettuce on each of 4 plates. Cut each sausaged egg lengthwise, and place 4 halves gently but firmly, yolk side up, on the lettuce. Neatly dispose 2 tomato slices on each plate. Stir sauce again, pour into a silver sauceboat. Serve the eggs and pass the sauce.

I suggest thin slices of hot or cold buttered pumpernickel as an accompaniment. You will want little else, except possibly a pitcher of cold beer or stout.

Pasta

Vermicelli Buonarroti

SERVES 4 OR 8

It is said, though I cannot confirm the saying, that this dish was created by Michelangelo while he was painting the mural depicting Hell in the Sistine Chapel. Whether true or not, the legend and the internal fire of the recipe itself make it eminently suitable for inclusion in this volume. As a main dish it will serve four; as a pasta course it will serve eight.

8 flat anchovy fillets	2 tablespoons minced
canned in oil	parsley
10 small green chili	¼ teaspoon cracked red
peppers	pepper
3 small dried red chili	¼ teaspoon cracked black
peppers	pepper
8 red pimentos	2 tablespoons tomato
3 garlic cloves	paste
1 cup olive oil	1 pound vermicelli
2 tablespoons kosher salt	

Remove anchovy fillets, whole, from the can and place on 2 layers of paper towels. Cover with another 2 layers and press gently, but firmly, to drain off oil. While anchovies drain, slice the green and red chili peppers very thin. Set aside 1 tablespoon chopped green pepper and 1 teaspoon red. Finely chop pimentos; peel and halve garlic. Chop drained anchovies coarsely.

In a large saucepan place 1 tablespoon olive oil and the salt. Put saucepan over medium flame and almost fill with water. Bring to a boil. While water heats, pour remaining olive oil into a large skillet and add to it all the chopped green and red peppers—except the reserved quantities—the parsley, pimentos, garlic, the cracked red and black pepper, and the tomato paste. Cook over a low heat but do not bring to a boil or even a simmer. Stir constantly. When water in saucepan starts to boil, put in the vermicelli, stir with a wooden spoon and add reserved chopped chili peppers. Stir again with wooden spoon and let spoon stay in saucepan to keep water from boiling over. Boil for 5 minutes. Taste. By now, pasta should be al dente. Drain but retain the chili peppers. Return vermicelli to saucepan, and add retained peppers. Pour contents of skillet over the pasta and mix the sauce well into the vermicelli. Serve at once.

Zucchini, eggplant, or any of half a dozen other vegetables go well with the vermicelli. The wine should be Italian, either red or white.

Penne Arrabbiate

SERVES 4 OR 8

Freely translated the title means "angry man's quill." Curiously, the dish is seldom found in Italy outside of Rome. Perhaps because that city boasts more angry men than does the rest of the country, excluding Sicily, of course. Penne arrabbiate is not too fiery, but is not for ulcer sufferers. If you follow the recipe below it makes an exhilarating main dish for four, or a pasta course for eight. One of my tasters felt that the sauce was too meager. This is a typical American reaction. In Italy pasta is not immersed in a sauce, but eaten with, rather than covered by it.

You *must* use proper Italian tomatoes. They are pear-shaped, smaller, and contain much less liquid than American tomatoes.

3½ pounds fresh Italian tomatoes	*4 tablespoons kosher salt*
1 tablespoon olive oil	*1 pound penne*
1 tablespoon butter	*4–8 tablespoons chopped parsley*
4 garlic cloves	
2 fresh Italian red chili peppers	

Skin tomatoes and dice coarsely. Heat oil and butter in a large heavy skillet. Cut garlic into halves and when oil and butter in skillet begin to simmer, add garlic. Cook until it starts to brown. Meanwhile cut red peppers into small bits, discarding seeds. Place in skillet, and simmer for 1 minute. Remove and discard garlic pieces. Remove skillet from heat. Place tomatoes in skillet and return to heat. Cook over low heat, stirring constantly with a wooden spoon, breaking up tomato dice as they cook, until you have a kind of a liquid paste. The cooking time should be about 15 minutes.

Meanwhile fill a 3-quart saucepan almost to the top with water, and add the salt. Put over medium heat. When water boils, add penne and stir. Boil pasta, stirring now and again, for 7 or 8 minutes or until it is al dente. Drain cooked pasta through a colander, then divide it onto hot plates and spoon some sauce over each portion. Sprinkle with the chopped parsley and serve.

Whether a main course or a pasta course, serve white Italian wine with it. One of my learned friends, cook, gourmet, who was also a taster, says he prefers ale or beer. This is his opinion, and you are welcome to it. The pasta should be preceded by an antipasto. Whatever you serve your guests, do *not* include grated cheese to sprinkle on the pasta.

Spaghetti Aglio e Olio

SERVES 4 OR 6

Some unknown Italian chef seems to have created a classic recipe specifically for this book. The dish, one of my quickest and easiest, will make a lunch for four hungry people or a pasta course for six.

Pasta comes in many forms. For this dish, and for variety, I used a kind known as *lingue di passeri piccole*: little sparrow's tongues. It is as long as regular spaghetti, but flatter and almost square in cross section.

3 tablespoons salt	*¾ cup olive oil*
1 pound lingue di passeri piccole	*1½ teaspoons cracked red pepper*
8 garlic cloves	

Pour 5 quarts of water into a large, wide saucepan or kettle. Add salt, cover, and bring to a boil. Put in the pasta, stir occasionally, and cook uncovered for about 8 minutes. Taste. If pasta is al dente, remove pot from fire, drain, and return pasta to kettle. (Eight minutes boiling should be sufficient, but if pasta is not done to your liking, boil another minute or so. Beware, however, of its becoming a soggy lump of glop.)

Meanwhile, as the water is coming to a boil and the pasta cooks, go to your chopping block. Peel the garlic cloves and, with a sharp knife, cleave the cloves into wafer-thin slices. Place the oil in a skillet and heat over a moderate flame. Put in garlic and cook until it turns golden. Sprinkle in the cracked pepper. Stir. Remove skillet from fire and allow the contents to relax until pasta is drained and back in its pot. Pour contents of skillet over pasta, and with your ever-reliable wooden spoon combine the sauce well with the pasta and serve it on hot plates. Immediacy is not a problem as the pasta can be kept warm over a very low flame or on a hot plate.

Spaghetti aglio e olio should be accompanied by wine. A Barolo is delicious. A mixed green salad, containing small lumps of avocado, commends itself if the pasta is the main offering. No matter when you serve this spaghetti, *never, never* sprinkle it with cheese.

Spaghetti alla Carbonara

SERVES 4

Not too far to the east of the Tiber lies an area known as the Abruzzi. It is famous for many things, including the beauty of its char-women—not the daily char but women who carry loads of wood for charcoal on their heads—and its extensive supplies of coal. The area also gives us a fine, fiery spaghetti which would have delighted Hell's caterers. Actually the dish originated with the charcoal burners. Far from their villages, they had to rely for food on basic local staples such as pasta, salt pork, and eggs.

After one experience in making the dish, you can repeat it in less than half an hour. Speed in the kitchen plus the fact that almost any larder contains the ingredients make it ideal for an impromptu lunch or supper.

6 rashers smoked bacon,
¼ inch thick
⅓ cup white Chianti
1 teaspoon freshly ground
black pepper
3 tablespoons kosher
(or sea) salt
1 pound spaghetti

3 whole eggs
2 egg yolks
1 cup freshly grated
parmesan cheese
1 tablespoon cracked
black pepper
¼ teaspoon salt

Cut bacon into squares and cook over slow heat in a skillet until the bacon is not quite done. Remove bacon and drain on paper towels. Discard all the bacon fat in skillet except for a thin veil to cover the bottom. Put wine in skillet and return bacon. Grate the fresh pepper over it. Bring to a boil, reduce heat, cover, and simmer about 5 minutes. Remove skillet to a warm place. To save time, you may pour about a gallon of water into a large pot, add kosher salt, and bring to a boil. Immerse the spaghetti. Meanwhile, place eggs, egg yolks, parmesan cheese, cracked black pepper, and salt in a mixing bowl and mix quietly with a balloon whisk. The eggs should be melded into the cheese, not beaten.

Now you are ready to combine all. Warm a large serving bowl or tureen, add the egg and cheese mixture. Drain the bacon and add it to the bowl. By now the spaghetti has cooked for about 8 minutes and should be done. Drain the pasta and toss it a bit to rid it of excess water. Add the spaghetti to the tureen and mix the whole as though you were being urged on by a minor but ambitious fiend with a sharp pitchfork. When the mixture is thoroughly wedded, serve at once.

Serve with it a bowl of grated parmesan and a good Chianti, either white or red. Wine is not the best coolant for the back taste of this spaghetti, but you cannot possibly eat bread with it and the wine does soothe the mouth and palate, if only temporarily.

Trenette con Pesto alla Genovese

SERVES 4 OR 8

In many fields Italians have a reputation for subtlety, and nowhere does their fine hand show more than in the flavoring of food. The sauce for this pasta enhances that reputation. Unlike many fiery dishes, pesto starts no blaze behind your palate after the first or second forkful. Not until you have eaten four or five do you realize that fire lurks in the sauce. Even then the flavor is more like the thrust of a stiletto than the blow of a broadsword. But the taste of garlic lingers on long after the pesto is finished. Because trenette con pesto alla genovese is comparatively mild it is one of the few dishes in this collection which may be safely served on the same menu with one or another of the recipes in this book.

Originally the sauce was prepared in a mortar and pestle. Sheer laziness and some impatience have led me to substitute a blender for the older kitchen implements. The recipe calls for trenette, a somewhat narrower noodle than fettuccine, but thicker. It is not always available. Substitute linguine, or even fettuccelle. The cheese, pecorino, made from goats' milk may also be difficult to find. In that case you may substitute romano.

3 tablespoons kosher salt
1 pound trenette
2 cups coarsely chopped
  fresh basil
¾ cup coarsely chopped
  fresh parsley
10 garlic cloves
1¾ cups freshly grated
  pecorino cheese

1½ cups olive oil
¼ cup Cinque Terre or
  other semisweet white
  wine
1 teaspoon freshly
  ground black pepper
Cayenne (optional)

Nearly fill a gallon kettle with water. Add the salt, cover, and place over high heat. When water boils, add pasta. Boil gently, stirring occasionally, until pasta is al dente, about 7 or 8 minutes. While water comes to a boil and pasta cooks, place basil and parsley in a blender. Peel and dice garlic; add to blender. Place 1¼ cups cheese in blender. Add olive oil, wine, and pepper; blend at high speed for about 2 minutes. The yield should be a fairly liquid paste—gooey, rather than runny. If too liquid add more cheese; if too thick, add more wine. Blend again. Contents of both blender and kettle should be finished at the same time.

As soon as the pasta is cooked, drain in a colander, and divide at once among the requisite number of very hot plates. Remove sauce from blender, and pour equal quantities of it on top of pasta. Sprinkle each serving very lightly with cayenne if desired. Place remaining grated cheese in a bowl that each diner may add cheese as he likes.

Whether you serve the pasta as a separate course or as the main course you should also serve with it a lightly chilled white wine. A simple salad of lettuce and cherry tomatoes with Italian dressing is a sufficient side dish.

Flaming Fettuccine

SERVES 6 OR 12

Anyone who has ever eaten fettuccine at the original Alfredo's in Rome will happily take oath that it is the ultimate in fettuccine, if not indeed in all pasta. To me, at least, this doubly fiery version is second only to that of the great maestro himself. In some measure it derives from Alfredo's as his fettuccine was frequently followed by a flaming omelet served to the accompaniment of lowered lights and soft Italian music from a violin. Flaming fettuccine is as appealing to the eye as it is to the taste.

The quantities below will make enough to serve six people amply as a main dish or twelve as a pasta course. (NOTE: in this recipe and in this one only, the word "Stock" refers to an Italian brandy and not to a broth.)

Sauce

8 tablespoons (1 stick) butter	½ cup Stock or cognac
2 tablespoons Worcestershire sauce	1 tablespoon chili powder
½ tablespoon Tabasco	¾ teaspoon freshly ground black pepper
	4 tablespoons sour cream

Melt butter in a small saucepan. Add Worcestershire, Tabasco, ¼ cup Stock or cognac, and chili powder; grind in the pepper and add the sour cream. Stir constantly over low heat until sauce is smooth. Do not allow the sauce to boil. Remove from heat. Cover and forget it while you prepare the fettuccine.

Pasta

¼ pound sliced prosciutto	2 green chili peppers
2 garlic cloves	2 dried red chili peppers
4 eggs	2 tablespoons salt
1 teaspoon freshly ground white pepper	1 tablespoon olive oil
⅓ cup grated parmesan cheese	1 pound fettuccine

Preheat the oven to 250 degrees.

Cut prosciutto into ½-inch squares. Peel and mince garlic. Break eggs into a large ovenproof bowl and beat gently with a wire whisk until they are a uniform shade of yellow. Add the prosciutto, garlic, white pepper, and cheese. Cut the green and red chili peppers in half; set aside. Fill a large kettle or saucepan with water; add salt, the chili peppers, and olive oil. Cover, bring to a boil. Put in the fettuccine and stir with a wooden spoon. Boil gently until pasta is al dente, 7 to 8 minutes. Stir the pasta a couple of times as it cooks. When done, remove chili peppers and drain fettuccine in a colander. Put pasta into bowl with egg and cheese mixture. Stir with a silver serving spoon and fork until the little ribbons have absorbed contents of bowl. Place bowl in the preheated oven to warm through while you finish the sauce. Pour reserved Stock or cognac into a small saucepan over low heat and put the saucepan with the sauce over another low burner. When Stock begins to bead at the edges, ignite and pour, flaming, into the sauce. While sauce still flames, remove fettuccine from oven and pour blazing sauce over it. Stir well until flames die and the sauce is an integral part of the dish. Serve at once.

With the fettuccine you need chilled white Soave. How much will depend on the wine-bibbing habits of your several guests. If the pasta be preceded by cold boiled artichokes with a vinaigrette sauce you will require no salad.

Three-Martini Cannelloni

SERVES 6

When I am working on a long or complex recipe I encourage myself with a martini now and then. This cannelloni is both long and complex, hence the title. *Prego*, do not skip it because of the time or work. The recipe is one of the best in the book, and will earn you both plaudits and kudos, which is, after all, why one cooks, is it not? Have four martinis if you like and have a good head, but do try it. If you do, you'll be hooked, and cannelloni will become one of your favorite dishes for entertaining.

Cannelloni is made in three parts. First make the pasta because it has to dry for an hour before cooking. During that hour you prepare the filling and make the sauce.

Pasta

2⅔ *cups hard flour*	*3 eggs*
Salt	

Sift flour and 1⅓ teaspoons salt into a bowl. Make a well in the flour. Beat 3 eggs lightly and pour gently into the well. Combine beaten eggs with flour by sprinkling latter lightly over the eggs and gradually working into a dough. Flour a wooden or marble bread board. Put the dough on the board and knead with the heel of your hand for 12 or 15 minutes. Divide dough in half. Flour a rolling pin and roll out each half of dough in turn until the dough is about ⅛ inch thick. Cut the dough into strips about 3 inches wide and put through the thinning rollers of a pasta machine several times, decreasing the thickness until your strips of pasta are about 1⁄16 inch thick. Cut the pasta into 4-inch squares and dry for 1 hour on paper towels.

Filling

1¼ pounds homemade Italian fiery bulk sausage	1 tablespoon cracked red pepper

While pasta dries, prepare the filling. Place the sausage in a bowl and knead in the cracked red pepper. Place sausage in a heavy skillet over low heat; stir, and turn constantly to avoid burning until sausage is done, about 10 minutes. After 5 minutes taste to see if sausage is sufficiently fiery. Remember the potency will be reduced by the pasta, sauce, cheese, and the cooking. Add more cracked red pepper if needed. When sausage is done pour off grease and return sausage to bowl until it is cool enough to handle.

Sauce

1 medium onion	¼ teaspoon ground sage
1 garlic clove	Salt
3 pounds fresh tomatoes	Freshly ground black
1 tablespoon olive oil	pepper
1½ tablespoons butter	1–2 tablespoons tomato
1 small bay leaf	paste (optional)

While the filling cools, make the sauce. Peel and finely dice the onion and place in a bowl. Peel garlic and put through a press. Add to the bowl. Peel, seed, and coarsely chop the tomatoes. Heat olive oil and 1½ tablespoons butter in a heavy skillet and add onion and garlic, cooking until onion is translucent. Add tomatoes and bring to a simmer. Add bay leaf and sage. Simmer uncovered for 20 minutes, mashing the tomatoes with a wooden spoon to make a thin paste. Taste and add salt and pepper as needed. If sauce seems acid, add a small pinch of sugar; if too liquid, thicken it with 1 or 2 tablespoons of tomato paste. Set aside.

Assembly

1 egg	12 ounces mozzarella
Butter	cheese

Beat egg lightly and mix into the sausage to bind the meat. Bring 2 quarts of salted water to a boil and lightly grease a baking pan with butter. Preheat oven to 350 degrees. Cut mozzarella into thin slices.

By now the pasta should be sufficiently dry to cook. Drop 2 or 3 squares at a time into the water; reduce water to a gentle boil and cook pasta for 3 minutes. Remove squares, plunge into a bowl of ice water (a vital step), and place on a damp dish towel to dry, turning once. Repeat process until all pasta has been cooked.

Mix another martini and prepare yourself for the final maneuvers. Arrange on each pasta square about 1 tablespoon of sausage filling, then fold the pasta over the filling to make a cannelloni roll. Place the rolls side by side, touching, in the buttered pan. Cover the rolls with the tomato sauce and arrange cheese slices on top. Bake for 20 minutes. Remove from oven, place under a hot broiler for another 2 to 3 minutes, or until cheese is slightly brown.

Precede the cannelloni by an antipasto and you need no salad. You could offer zabaglione or a flaming omelette soufflé for dessert. Serve red Valpolicella throughout.

CURRIES

To write a book about fiery food without a section on curries would be a nullity. Not all curries are fiery but most are, and I have tried to present representative samples of the fiery ones. This is a selection, not a compendium of curries; a compendium would require three volumes each the size of this one. I confess to omitting the ferociously hot tamil curries of Ceylon. Ability to enjoy or even eat these red curries has to be imbibed with one's mother's milk.

Generally speaking curries are, like Burnside's army before Fredericksburg, divided into three grand divisions. They are: sweet curries, largely from Thailand, Burma, and Indonesia; dry curries, and liquid or sauced curries from India, Ceylon, parts of the Middle East, and Indonesia. Sweet curries, having scant fire, are unacceptable for this book. The difference between dry curries and liquid ones is simple. Nearly all curries are served with rice. With dry curries the rice is cooked as an integral part of the dish. With liquid curries the rice is cooked separately and the curry is spooned on top of it. Dry curries are also known as "pellews," "pootoos," and "pulaos."

In India cooks grind their own spice mixtures daily. Combinations are almost infinite. Garam Masala, "hot spices," so called because they are supposed to provide body heat, consists of a tablespoon each of: cardamom pods, whole cloves, black cumin seeds, black peppercorns, and cinnamon; and ¼ teaspoon each of nutmeg and mace. These are ground together in a mortar. This yields a good quantity of seasoning and strong, too. Grinding it by hand is a tiresome job. Fortunately you can buy all the ingredients already ground and combine them, but the result will not be so strong. By altering, or adding to the list of spices, by using fenugreek or coriander, for example, you can greatly change the taste of the curry.

The spices and other ingredients in curry powder, in addition to those already mentioned are anise, mustard and poppy seeds, allspice, almonds, coconut and coconut milk, garlic, onions, ginger, lime juice, vinegar, curry leaves (substitute bay), mangoes, saffron, and turmeric.

Experiment and experience guided by sagacity will permit you to "roll your own," so to speak, and produce many different varieties and tastes. When curry powder appears in a recipe in this book, however, I am calling for commercial curry powder. In the first place, curry powder is used in recipes other than curries per se and to get the same effect each time, the recipe ingredients must be uniform. Secondly, you may not be able to find the necessary spices to make curry powder, and thirdly, you will be saved a lot of kitchen time and work. Whether you make your own curry powder or buy it, remember that it loses, as do we all, its virtue with age. Keep it well stoppered.

Remember, too, that freshly made curry powder is considerably stronger than commercial and should be used accordingly. Remember finally, that to give real flavor and fire to a dish, *all* curry powder *must* be cooked into the dish and not merely stirred into it.

With most recipes I have tried to suggest a wine or other beverage suitable to the dish. Curries present a perplexing problem. Most of them come from countries whose population is predominately Moslem or Hindu. To both alcohol is forbidden, hence little indigenous wine exists. I enjoy beer, or ale with curry, or even a rough red wine. I have tried to make suggestions suitable to wine bibbers.

Lastly: be not dismayed by the number of the ingredients and length of instructions of a curry recipe. Recall what Ogden Nash might have written:

> Never hurry
> A curry.

Dry Curry of Lamb Mysore

SERVES 4

This recipe comes from the southern part of Kipling's India, and calls for mutton. I have suggested lamb because mutton is extremely hard to find even at the best butcher stalls. Should you be more fortunate and have mutton available, use it. Remember, however, that the cooking time for mutton is an hour, rather than twenty minutes, before you add the rice.

One essential point: be sure that your butcher gives you *lean* lamb, preferably from a leg. Such lamb will cost you more than other cuts, but the result is worth the expense. Too much fat in this dish would ruin it.

1 medium onion
1 medium carrot
1 celery rib with leaves
3 parsley sprigs
6 whole black
  peppercorns
1 teaspoon salt
1½ pounds lamb bones,
  with attached meat
8 dried red chili peppers
2 1-inch pieces fresh
  ginger, ½-inch thick
1 teaspoon cumin seed
6 whole cloves
1 tablespoon cider
  vinegar
2 teaspoons vegetable oil

2 tablespoons curry
  powder
6 garlic cloves
1 tablespoon sugar
1 teaspoon salt
2 pounds lean lamb, cut
  into 1-inch cubes
1 green bell pepper
½ cup dry-roasted
  peanuts
1 tomato
1 cup rice
Mango chutney
Red pepper relish
Hot fruit chutney
Mustard pickles

Make the stock first, preferably the night before you plan to cook the dish, or at least early enough in the morning to refrigerate until fat rises to the top and makes a stiff layer which can easily be removed. To make stock: peel and quarter onion; scrape and dice carrot; chop celery and leaves coarsely. Place all in a large—3-quart or more—heavy saucepan. Add parsley, peppercorns, salt, lamb bones, and water to cover contents. Set over low heat and simmer 2 hours. Remove from heat. Strain and discard all solids. Let cool. Place in refrigerator until fat rises to top and solidifies. Skim off fat and discard it.

Chop chili peppers small, saving half the seeds. Scrape and dice ginger. Put ginger and chili peppers in a blender. Add cumin, cloves, and vinegar. Blend 30 seconds at moderately high speed. Drain off liquid and put the remaining solids from the blender in a square of cheesecloth to make a bouquet garni. Pour vegetable oil into a small saucepan, heat, and add curry powder. Cook, stirring continually, until curry turns brown. Remove from heat. Mash garlic, or put it through a press. Place bouquet garni, cooked curry powder, garlic, sugar, and salt into a large heavy saucepan with a tight lid. Mix well and add lamb cubes. Pour in strained lamb stock, bring to a boil, reduce heat, cover, and simmer 20 minutes. While lamb cooks, remove seeds and membranes from green pepper and cut into small dice. Cut peanuts into quarters. Skin tomato and quarter. At the end of 20 minutes add rice to saucepan, stir well, re-cover and simmer 15 minutes. Check to see if more liquid is needed. If so, add a little water. By the end of another 15 minutes, the rice should have absorbed all the liquid and be soft and fluffy. Remove contents of skillet to a hot serving dish. Sprinkle with the chopped green pepper and peanuts. Garnish with tomato wedges and serve.

In separate dishes, place mango chutney, red pepper relish, hot fruit chutney, and mustard pickles. For those who like their curry very fiery, add a small bowl of Penang Chili Sauce (page 165). Any or all of these relishes may be placed on top of the curry and mixed into it, or be used individually on each forkful.

For those who do not like beer, I suggest a rather rough, red wine, made from the Gamay grape. A green salad with a few arti-choke hearts and cucumber chunks is becoming to the curry, with or after it.

Vegetable Curry

SERVES 4

Except for the Sikhs, Hindus do not eat meat. But they do eat many curries made exclusively with vegetables. I have eaten some of them, and even to a carnivore like me the absence of meat is virtually impossible to detect. Where meat is expensive, this curry provides a fine substitute. The use of almonds, a low-cost item in India, does raise the price in this country, but you will still find vegetable curry an inexpensive way to entertain, and entertain well.

The following recipe does not make for a really fiery dish, say a two-alarmer. By adding more whole cloves, cardamom, and fenugreek you can add another alarm.

1½ cups rice
2 large onions
2 garlic cloves
1 cup vegetable oil
½ teaspoon shredded
   saffron
½ teaspoon salt
12 whole cloves
4 teaspoons ground
   cardamom
4 teaspoons fenugreek
8 whole allspice

¾ cup shelled almonds
1 large green bell
   pepper
2 celery ribs
1 tablespoon butter
4 tablespoons seedless
   raisins
Hot mustard pickle
Mango chutney
Sweet pepper relish
Hot tomato relish

Place rice in a closely woven strainer. Wash thoroughly in cold running water and allow to drain. Peel both onions and mince one. Cut the other in half and slice thinly. Put onions in separate bowls and set aside. Peel and mash both garlic cloves. Place oil in a large heavy skillet over moderate heat, add minced onion and garlic. Cook, stirring occasionally, until onion is soft, but neither onion nor garlic is brown. Meanwhile, put saffron into a bowl containing 1½ cups water, stir, and set aside. When onion is cooked, add rice to skillet. Put in salt, cloves, cardamom, fenugreek, allspice, and saffron water. Cover skillet and simmer 20 minutes, or until rice is dry and fluffy.

While rice cooks, fill a small saucepan with water, bring to a boil; add almonds, remove from stove and let cool until almonds can be handled comfortably. Remove skins and set almonds aside. Remove seeds and membranes from green pepper and cut into julienne strips. Cut strips in half. Add to bowl with sliced onion. Cut celery into 1-inch squares and put in same bowl. Melt butter in a small saucepan. Add the skinned almonds and the raisins. Cook, stirring frequently, until raisins have puffed and almonds have started to brown. By now rice should be dry and fluffy, and contents of skillet done. Put both on a hot serving platter. Add the sliced onion, green pepper, celery squares, almonds, and raisins. Serve at once.

In separate bowls place: hot mustard pickle, mango chutney, sweet pepper relish, and hot tomato relish. Pass the bowls around the table for individual selection.

Strong Darjeeling tea is the obvious drink with this dish. A basket of fresh fruit will not only provide a good end to the meal, but will also eliminate the need for salad, which is seldom served with a curry, especially a dry one.

Curried Chicken in Casserole

SERVES 6

Seldom should curries be cooked in casseroles, but this one is. Although you should allow two days to prepare and cook this curry, you can do it in one if you get up early enough. The advantage of the casserole, albeit untraditional, is that you will have the last hour of cooking to gossip and drink with your guests. After the first mouthful or so you may wonder why this curry is included in a fiery cookbook. By the time you have finished the meal any doubts will be put at rest.

I have adjusted the recipe for two-day cooking, that you may let the stock rest overnight and remove the fat more easily and not burn your fingers cutting up the chicken.

2 chicken breasts, split   *4 chicken thighs*
4 chicken legs   *5 cups chicken stock*

Wash chicken pieces and discard any loose skin. Place stock in a large saucepan, add chicken, cover, and simmer until chicken is done (about 50 minutes, depending on size and age of chicken). Drain chicken, reserving stock. Place chicken and stock in separate bowls and refrigerate. Hours later, or the next day, remove and discard bones and skin from chicken and cut meat into bite-size pieces. Set aside. Remove congealed fat and reserve stock.

2 meduim onions	½ teaspoon ground
3 tablespoons vegetable	cinnamon
oil	½ teaspoon freshly
2 garlic cloves	ground black pepper
2 tablespoons curry	1 medium green bell
powder	pepper
1 teaspoon ground	8 scallions
cumin	1½ cups raw rice
1 teaspoon salt	½ cup coconut juice
2 teaspoons ground	Grated coconut
ginger	Green tomato chutney
½ teaspoon ground cloves	Shredded almonds

Preheat the oven to 400 degrees.

Peel and chop onions. Place vegetable oil in a heavy skillet over low heat and add chopped onions. Cook until translucent, stirring as necessary to prevent burning. Meanwhile peel garlic and mince or put through a press. Place in a bowl. Add to bowl all other ingredients down to and including the black pepper. Mix thoroughly. When onions are done, add contents of bowl to skillet, stir onions into the spices, and continue to cook, again stirring to prevent burning. While contents of skillet cook until mixture is dark brown, remove seeds and membranes from green pepper and dice coarsely. Slice scallions into ¼-inch pieces. Place chopped peppers and scallions in separate serving bowls to be used as garnish.

Place chopped chicken into a serving casserole. Sprinkle rice over it. Add contents of skillet, 2½ cups of the reserved chicken stock, and the coconut juice. Mix well. Cover and place in preheated oven for 1 hour. Serve from casserole.

With this curry you should serve in individual bowls: grated coconut, green tomato chutney, shredded almonds, and a chutney sauce without solid pieces of fruit. Let each diner add to his curry his own selection of condiments. A chilled Piesporter would be an acceptable wine, if you don't like beer.

Curried Scrambled Eggs

SERVES 4

Curried scrambled eggs are light, and require few accompanying condiments. They are more adapted to lunch or supper than to dinner. Although not included in the original Indian recipe, I added bacon to this version. The taste of the bacon adds to the taste of the whole.

1 cup raw rice
1 tablespoon salt
1 medium large onion
6 tablespoons butter
3 tablespoons curry
powder
3 10-ounce cans concen-
trated tomato soup
1½ teaspoons ground
ginger

1 teaspoon ground
cinnamon
1 large tart apple
1¼ tablespoons diced
cooked bacon
9 eggs
Mango chutney
Hot mustard pickles

Place rice in a large saucepan almost full of boiling salted water. Let rice boil, stirring twice with a wooden spoon which you leave in the pot to prevent its boiling over. While rice cooks, about 20 minutes, chop onion. Melt 4 tablespoons butter in a heavy 2-quart saucepan. Add onion and cook over low heat until it is soft. Remove and reserve onion. Add remaining butter, bring almost to a simmer, and put in curry powder. Cook, stirring occasionally until curry has turned brown. Return onion to saucepan and add tomato soup, ginger, and cinnamon. While contents of saucepan are brought to a simmer, core, but do not peel apple, and cut into large dice. Add to saucepan. Cover and simmer for 10 or 12 minutes, until sauce is smooth. Sprinkle in the bacon and stir. Cover and simmer another 5 minutes.

Break eggs into a bowl and beat firmly but gently with a balloon whisk until eggs are smooth and light yellow. Fold the eggs slowly into the saucepan, stirring constantly with the whisk. Continue to stir over a low heat until the eggs are scrambled, the contents of the saucepan are even in texture, and the eggs well set. Remove to a warm place. Divide the cooked rice into 4 portions, cover with the scrambled eggs and serve on hot plates.

Provide mango chutney and hot mustard pickles in side dishes. If you want to be fancy, a side dish of dried, flaked codfish would add a distinctive flavor. A small salad of diced cooked beets and cucumber on a bed of shredded lettuce would be good with or after the curry. Tea goes well with the eggs.

Curried Chicken Livers

SERVES 2

If you crave culinary esteem without long hours slaving over a hot stove this is a good dish with which to impress your guest. With a little preliminary work in the kitchen, you can cook these livers at the table in a chafing dish. The procedure not only gives you a chance to show off your skill but also allows you to spend with your friend the time you would otherwise be alone in the kitchen. If you wish to impress three guests, double the quantities below. No condiments such as bananas, coconut, chutney, or Bombay duck are required. The curry is comparatively mild, and condiments would only detract from the delicate taste of the livers.

1 pound fresh chicken livers	*4 teaspoons curry powder*
1 medium onion	*4 teaspoons sifted flour*
2 tablespoons vegetable oil	*1 cup rich chicken stock*

Wash, clean livers, and mince onion in the kitchen. Dry livers between towels. Heat oil in a chafing dish blazer pan. Add onion, stirring occasionally to prevent burning. Cook over moderate heat until onion begins to color. Remove from skillet to a warm plate. Put chicken livers in pan and lightly brown on all sides. Remove livers and keep warm. As the livers cook, mix the curry powder and flour in a small bowl. Put the curry-flour mixture into the skillet and cook it in the residue remaining until the mixture is brown. Now add the stock; stir well and make into a sauce which should be on the thin side. Return livers and onions to blazer pan, cover, and simmer 15 minutes. Stir now and again to coat the livers well. Taste for salt. Recover pan and simmer another 5 minutes. The livers are now ready.

You may serve them over toast points or over rice. A dish of skinned, sliced tomatoes, sprinkled with chopped parsley and seasoned with salt and pepper makes an ideal accompaniment to the livers.

The Major's Kidneys

SERVES 4

Why is it that almost all British officers who retired from the Indian Army did so with the rank of major? Perhaps those who did not retire went on to become brigadiers. No doubt someday someone will write a learned monograph on the subject. He will probably be some young swot down from Cambridge. No matter. The recipe comes from a retired major who had served for years with the Gurkha Rifles, little men in green uniforms who carry rifles but prefer the kukri. But to return to the major's kidneys.

I met the major through a mutual friend on a P & O vessel. When I reached London, I forwarded my note of introduction and received an invitation to lunch at his cottage, "Kim's Cannon," near Stoke Poges. There he fed me his famous kidneys and gave me the recipe.

1 medium onion	*1 cup beef stock*
3 tablespoons butter	*2 teaspoons arrowroot*
16 lamb kidneys	*(if needed)*
3 tablespoons curry	*2 tablespoons chopped*
powder	*parsley*

Peel and mince onion. Melt butter in a heavy skillet, and add onion. Cook, stirring from time to time, until the onion takes on color. Remove as much suet from the kidneys as possible without deforming them, and cut crosswise into thirds. When onions are done add curry powder and cook until it is brown. Add kidneys, and brown on all sides. Pour in stock, and simmer uncovered for 20 minutes. If sauce is too thin, as is probable, put arrowroot into a small bowl, dip 2 tablespoons juice from the skillet and add to arrowroot to make a paste. Gradually mix paste into contents of the skillet to thicken sauce. Cover, and simmer another 10 minutes. By this time the kidneys will be done and the sauce should be sufficiently thick. Place kidneys on hot plates or in a hot tureen, and sprinkle them with parsley. Serve *now*.

With the dish offer 4 skinned and quartered tomatoes on a bed of endive—Major Buffington called it chicory—with a dollop of mayonnaise on the tomatoes and salt and pepper on the side. Hot buttered toast is a welcome accompaniment to the kidneys.

Curried Prawns

SERVES 4

To paraphrase a famous American expatriate who identified a rose with one iteration and one reiteration: a prawn is a prawn is a shrimp. To interpret for you: a prawn in England is what Americans call a jumbo shrimp. What the English call a shrimp so do we, but these are the little shrimp from the Gulf of Mexico and the waters of Florida, Georgia, and North Carolina. For this dish, you require prawns, or jumbo shrimp. They must be raw, preferably unfrozen, and in their own carapaces, which are needed for the sauce.

The following curried prawns will not kick you in the stomach like a mule, or torture your throat, but they contain some fire so treat them with the respect they deserve.

2 small onions	*3 tablespoons cornstarch*
2 carrots	*1 garlic clove*
6 black peppercorns	*1 teaspoon ground*
3 parsley sprigs	*ginger*
1 celery rib with leaves	*¾ cup raw rice*
Juice of 1 lemon	*½ cup fresh mango juice*
1 teaspoon salt	*(2 ripe mangoes)*
1¼ pounds raw jumbo	*Major Grey's chutney*
shrimp	*Mustard pickles*
¼ cup vegetable oil	*Diced hot pepper relish*
1 teaspoon dry mustard	*Diced red radishes*
3 tablespoons curry	
powder	

Peel and quarter 1 onion; peel and mince the other and set each aside separately. Cut 1 carrot into small rounds. Place 2 quarts water in a heavy saucepan, add quartered onion, sliced carrot, peppercorns, parsley, the celery leaves, lemon juice, and 1 teaspoon salt. Bring water to a boil. Add shrimp, cover, and simmer 5 minutes. Remove shrimp and place under cold running water until cool. Peel shrimp. Place shells in the saucepan with the shrimp stock and reduce to 1½ cups.

Meanwhile, place oil in a large skillet over low heat. When oil is hot, add dry mustard and minced onion, and cook slowly until onion is translucent. Blend curry and cornstarch. When onion has cooked remove contents of skillet and set them aside. Replace them with the curry powder-cornstarch mixture. Cover and simmer 3 minutes. Skin and mash garlic clove. Dice remaining carrot and the celery rib. Now start boiling the rice.

Return cooked onion to skillet. Add ginger, garlic, diced carrot, and celery. Strain contents of saucepan, discarding solids, and pour stock into the skillet. Over low heat blend contents until smooth, add shrimp, cover and simmer 10 minutes, or until mixture is thoroughly hot. Squeeze mangoes for juice and add to skillet.

The rice and the curry should be done at about the same time. Serve rice in one bowl, or tureen, and curry in another. Present rice first, that your guests may cover it with the curry. Provide side dishes of Major Grey's chutney, mustard pickles, diced hot pepper relish, and diced red radishes.

A chilled, dry, not too svelte, white wine is attractive with this curry. Follow the curry with a bowl of fresh fruit, and a selection of cheese.

Veal Curry Myrtle Hill

SERVES 4

Among our friends are two whose estate, Myrtle Hill, lies on Big Pipe Creek about fifteen miles north of Frederick, which in spring and summer is "green walled by the hills of Maryland". Recently they entertained for a week an eleven-year-old grandson. Although he is highly allergic to 57 varieties of vegetables, herbs, and spices, he can, if he chooses, safely eat the leaves of poison ivy. On pain of being bedridden for at least 48 hours, he must avoid: garlic, onions, all peppers, ginger, mustard, curry powder, and its individual components. Both his grandparents are redoubtable trenchermen and fond of spices. That they fed the lad and ate with him three meals a day for seven days is reminiscent of one of the labors of Heracles.

We arranged with our friends to dine with us when they brought the youth to Washington to catch his plane home. That morning's post brought a plaintive plea. The grandmother confirmed our dinner engagement and added: ". . . garlic, in Hell's name garlic, hot spices, and nuts; the bland food has done us in." Among other dishes I gave them this curry, hence its name. It was a simple meal with but six side dishes. Some made the curry more fiery, others partly masked the fire. The side dishes were: cooked, chopped bacon, ground almonds, Major Grey's mild chutney, sliced bananas, and Indonesian Cucumber Salad (page 157). Available also was a platter of sliced pumpernickel. Need I add that the curry was accompanied by boiled rice?

Ask your butcher to remove all fat and gristle from the veal and cut it into 1-inch cubes.

1 large onion	*2 teaspoons ground ginger*
5 tablespoons butter	*1 green apple*
2 pounds veal cubes, fat	*2 cups rich chicken stock*
and gristle removed	*1 tablespoon arrowroot*
3 garlic cloves	*1 tablespoon salt*
2 tablespoons curry powder	*2 tablespoons lemon juice*

Mince onion. Melt butter in a large skillet and cook onion, stirring to prevent burning, until onion starts to turn brown. Remove onion to a separate small bowl, put veal into skillet and brown meat on all sides. While veal cooks, mince garlic. Mix it with the curry powder and ginger. Transfer veal to another bowl, put mixture into the same skillet and stir well. Cover and simmer for about 10 minutes, during which time core, but do not peel apple, and mince. Return onion, and veal to skillet. Add apple, stock, arrowroot, and salt. Re-cover skillet and simmer contents for about 1 hour or until meat is tender. Just before serving, mix in the lemon juice and continue to simmer for 1 minute.

Chicken Curry XVI

SERVES 6

This curry bears some relation to the rijsttafel of Indonesia. The relationship, however, is about that of a third cousin thrice removed —sometimes one wishes that all cousins were totally removed—but it does have many side dishes. Hence the sixteen in the title. Most curries have fewer condiments. Like the curries of Thailand, which are sweet, rijsttafel is seldom fiery. Curry XVI burns.

For the economical or lazy chef, this curry has two advantages. It is made with leftover chicken and requires scant time or effort. The dish, including the chopping, can be made from scratch in about 90 minutes. The recipe should be read twice before you start, especially if you seek to set a record for speed, a deplorable objective in the kitchen. The best way to prepare the dish is to start backwards. Cook and chop most of the condiments first. Place them in small dishes and set aside until needed. For these side dishes you will need:

8 rashers bacon
2 eggs
6 pieces Bombay duck
6 scallions
1 cucumber
½ cup diced fresh
   pineapple

1 cup shelled almonds
2 tomatoes
1 eight-ounce can button
   mushrooms
1 cup crystallized ginger
1 cup minced parsley

Fry bacon in a large skillet until almost done. Remove bacon and drain on paper towels, reserving fat in skillet. Mince bacon. Hard cook eggs and place in refrigerator to cool. Bake Bombay duck in a medium oven until puffed and crisp. Cut into squares. Mince scallions. Wash, peel, and dice cucumber. Chop almonds coarsely. Skin and chop tomatoes. Quarter mushrooms, and dice ginger. Just before serving the curry, shell eggs, and slice finely. For the curry itself you will need:

1 large onion
1 large green bell pepper
1 small apple
2½ pounds cooked chicken
1 teaspoon cracked red
   pepper

5 tablespoons sifted flour
4½ tablespoons curry
   powder
4 cups chicken stock
Salt
2½ cups long-grain rice

Peel and chop onion. Remove seeds and membranes from green pepper and dice. Do not peel apple but core and chop enough to make 4 tablespoons. Cut enough chicken into 1-inch cubes to make 5 cups. Place skillet with reserved bacon drippings over medium heat and when fat is hot, add onion and green pepper. Cook until onion is translucent. Meanwhile, mix cracked red pepper, flour, and curry powder in a bowl. When onion is done add apple and cook another 2 minutes. Sprinkle bowl mixture into contents of skillet and, stirring constantly, cook about 3 minutes. Pour in stock to make a sauce, starting with 1 cup and, as sauce thickens, add more stock until you have the desired consistency. It should not be runny, nor too thick. Taste, and add salt as needed. Put in chicken, cover, and simmer for about 30 minutes. While you have been slaving at all the above chores with your right hand, with your left boil the rice in a large quantity of lightly salted water until it is fluffy.

You have made the curry and the rice is ready. You have prepared 11 side dishes, but need 5 more. Three come out of jars or cans and 2 must be prepared at the last moment.

1 cup mango chutney   *1 cup raisins*
1 cup grated coconut   *4 ripe, but firm bananas*
½ cup black currant jelly
2 tablespoons vegetable
  oil

Put chutney, coconut, and jelly into separate dishes and place with the other condiments. Heat oil in a small skillet, toss in the raisins and cook slowly until plump. Keep warm until placed on the table. While raisins cook, peel and thinly slice the bananas. Now you have to get your guests to the table and serve.

Pass the rice first, and follow with the curry. Arrange the side

dishes so that they may pass, as does port, from left to right around the table. Thus no guest misses a dish, and no guest receives the same dish twice. At least not until the rice and curry are passed a second time.

As this is not a pukka curry I omit pappadums, but substitute pumpernickel. Chicken Curry XVI is a one-dish meal, but if you want to make the occasion more festive, a thin soup would make an acceptable first course, with a simple tossed salad to follow. Then coffee.

Curried Canard

SERVES 6

Originally I wrote this theatrical recipe as a play in four acts and two intermissions, one for drink. The play was in the best tradition of a Greek tragedy—you ate the dramatis personae at the end—and, like the Attic drama, it was highly complex. This straightforward version is still complex, and must be divided into sections to prevent your getting lost in a labyrinth of ingredients, many of which recur in different parts of the recipe. Do not take the dish lightly. It requires about six hours to prepare and cook and the recipe should be read carefully at least thrice before you start work.

First you must cook the duck and make the stock.

1 five-pound duck	*15–20 black peppercorns*
3 large garlic cloves	*½ teaspoon cumin seed*
2 medium onions	*5 cardamom pods*
1 large carrot	*1 teaspoon whole*
2 celery ribs including	*coriander seeds*
leaves	*1 piece fresh ginger,*
2 parsley sprigs	*½-inch wide and*
5 tablespoons kosher salt	*1-inch long*

Place duck in a large soup kettle or saucepan. Cover with 10 to 12 cups cold water. Place, covered, over low heat. Coarsely chop and add to the kettle: garlic, onions, carrot, and celery. Add, too, the parsley, salt, peppercorns, cumin, cardamom, coriander seeds, and the ginger. Simmer slowly for 1½ hours, skimming occasionally. While duck cooks, make the basis for the marinade.

6 tablespoons olive oil
3 tablespoons curry
   powder
1 teaspoon ground cumin
¼ teaspoon ground
   turmeric
1 teaspoon ground
   cardamom

7 garlic cloves
1 onion
1 teaspoon freshly ground
   black pepper
⅔ cup cider vinegar

Heat oil in a skillet and add curry, cumin, turmeric, and cardamom. Simmer them until they turn dark, but stir often to prevent burning. While they cook, peel and mash garlic; peel and slice onion. Reserve contents of skillet.

When duck has cooked its allotted time, remove from kettle and allow to cool. Strain the liquid in which it simmered, discard all solids, and refrigerate the stock. When duck is cool enough to handle, remove meat from skin and bones. Discard the latter two, and cut meat into bite-size chunks. Place duck chunks in a bowl. Add reserved contents of skillet, the mashed garlic, sliced onion, pepper, and cider vinegar. Mix contents of bowl thoroughly now and again, and marinate duck for 2 hours.

While away the time as you please: have a drink, read other recipes, or go for a walk. At the end of the 2 hours you start the ultimate stage of this composition. First skim and discard the fat from the duck stock.

2 tablespoons arrowroot
2½ cups raw rice
1 green bell pepper
1 cup raisins
1 cup minced scallions
2 tablespoons peanut oil

1 cup roasted, slivered
   almonds
1 cup tomato-onion
   chutney
1 cup mango chutney

Place duck and its marinade in a large, heavy saucepan or the original soup kettle. Put kettle, covered, over medium heat. When marinade comes to a boil, slowly add the chilled and skimmed duck stock. Bring kettle to a boil again, reduce heat, and simmer 1½ hours.

If, after that time, the sauce is too thin, thicken with arrowroot. Mix it with 4 tablespoons of the sauce to make a paste, and gradually add to sauce in kettle, stirring constantly. Now start boiling the rice. Twenty minutes before serving, seed and remove membranes from green pepper and julienne it. Add to the kettle and cook another 10 minutes.

Rice should now be done. Cook raisins in peanut oil until they pop. Serve rice first, followed by curried canard and the bowls of condiments including: scallions, raisins, almonds, and the chutneys.

In addition you should have available Syrian flat bread, or chapati, an Indian flat bread made of whole wheat flour. Chilled strawberries would make a good dessert. As a drink you might try a full-bodied red wine or perhaps hot sake.

Pondicherry Curried Ham

SERVES 4

A recipe from southern India for curried ham could have been devised only by an Englishman, probably a minor civil servant when India was an important part of the Empire. Moslems may not eat pork of any kind, and Hindus are strict vegetarians. I suggest that

the composer of this curry was a minor civil servant because otherwise he would have taken to the hills when the weather was hot. Curry is a hot weather dish, and suitable for Pondicherry in summer. I have long rejected the idea of ham curry because I thought that the strong taste of ham would extirpate the taste of the curry. These doubts were illusionary, as my test of this recipe proved. Note that the recipe contains no commercial curry powder.

If your refrigerator, larder, or pantry contains a baked ham or part of one, use it. If not, your nearest delicatessen can supply half-inch-thick slices of baked smoked ham. You might find, too, canned or frozen grated coconut.

1¼ cups raw rice
1 cup grated coconut
1¼ cups milk
4 slices baked smoked ham
1 medium onion
2 tablespoons vegetable oil
2 tablespoons coriander seeds
1 teaspoon mustard seeds
1 teaspoon ground ginger
1 teaspoon fenugreek seeds

2 teaspoons ground turmeric
1 teaspoon freshly ground black pepper
¼ teaspoon cayenne
1 teaspoon cumin seeds
1 teaspoon chili powder
1 tablespoon white wine vinegar
1¼ tablespoons red currant jelly
2 garlic cloves, minced
Tomato chutney
Mustard pickles
Red pepper relish

Boil rice according to your custom. Put grated coconut in a bowl and pour milk over it. Allow to steep for at least 1 hour as you prepare other ingredients. Remove edges and fat from ham and cut it into ½-inch cubes. Set aside. Chop onion. Heat oil in a large, heavy saucepan or skillet. Put in onion and cook over a low heat, disturbing occasionally with a wooden spoon, until onion is translucent. While onion cooks, mix in a bowl the coriander, mustard seeds, ginger, fenugreek, turmeric, black pepper, cayenne, cumin seeds, and chili powder. Stir well. If you have a grinder, put the spices in it and reduce to a powder. Lacking a grinder you can use a mortar and pestle.

Return spice mixture to a bowl and set aside. The onions should now be cooked. Remove from pan and reserve. Put the spices in remaining oil and cook over a low heat, stirring often until they are dark brown. Return onion to the pan and remove from heat. Place a double layer of cheesecloth in a kitchen strainer over a small bowl. Put the steeped coconut into the strainer and squeeze out all the liquid, reserving both that and the coconut left in the strainer.

Add to saucepan the cubed ham, 1 cup coconut milk, 3 table-spoons grated coconut from strainer, vinegar, and jelly, together with the ground spices and cooked onion. Peel garlic and mince. Add to the saucepan. Mix garlic well with contents of pan, and place over medium heat. Simmer uncovered for about 30 minutes so that all is hot through and the liquid in the pan has been reduced to a thickish sauce.

Serve curry over rice and add as side dishes: tomato chutney, mustard pickles, and red pepper relish. Additional grated coconut may also be served on the side as well as a pair of thinly sliced bananas. For those who do not like beer or ale, I suggest tea, or a dry red wine.

A Borderline Curry

SERVES 6

I use the word "borderline" here in three senses. The recipe comes from the northwestern frontier of India bordering on Afghanistan. The dish is almost a sweet curry and hence not so fiery as those from the south—and thus a borderline case for inclusion in a book on fiery dishes. Finally it is made with beef, which is not my favorite meat for curry. I include the recipe only because beef is so much a part of the American scene, and many families frequently have left-over beef in their refrigerators. Finally, the dish is an authentic curry, and easy to make.

I have increased the quantity of curry powder and ginger to add more fire. If you want a sweet curry, cut the amount of ginger in half and replace half the curry powder with flour, and add a half cup of raisins to the skillet just before you simmer its contents.

1 large onion
1½ tablespoons butter
3 tablespoons vegetable oil
½ teaspoon ground cinnamon
2 teaspoons ground ginger
1 teaspoon ground coriander
1 teaspoon ground cloves
2 garlic cloves
2 pounds top round of beef, ground twice

1 tablespoon salt
1½ cups raw rice
1 tablespoon flour
2¼ tablespoons curry powder
¾ cup beef stock
½ cup coconut juice
Mango chutney
Grated coconut
Diced sweet pepper relish
Penang Chili Sauce (page 165)

Peel onion and mince. Place half the butter and half the oil in a large heavy skillet over low heat. When it begins to simmer, add minced onion, and cook, turning from time to time until onion is transparent. Mix the cinnamon, ginger, coriander, and cloves in a bowl. Mince garlic and add to bowl. Stir well. By now the onion should be sufficiently cooked. Remove from skillet with a slotted spoon and set aside. Place contents of bowl in skillet and add ground meat, stirring to combine meat with other ingredients, and cook it until brown on all sides.

While meat simmers, bring 2 quarts of water to a boil in a large saucepan. Put in salt and add rice. Stir with a wooden spoon and let boil slowly, uncovered. Now and again, stir rice. Heat remaining oil and butter in another saucepan. Mix flour and curry powder and put into saucepan to make a paste. After it has cooked about 5 minutes gradually add the beef stock and the coconut juice. Continue to cook over low heat until you have a sauce of medium consistency. Pour the sauce over the ground beef in the skillet and mix well. Drain the rice and wash it well with cold water. Continue to heat and stir beef in skillet.

Serve rice first, followed immediately by the beef curry. With the main dish serve the relishes and condiments that each diner may season his own curry.

A salad of lettuce, halved red and yellow cherry tomatoes, and a few chopped scallions might well accompany or follow the curry. Beer, naturally.

NONCURRIES

One of the philosophical dicta which I picked up in a course on logic was that all the world could be divided between coal scuttles and noncoal scuttles. This bit of lore has not been of much use to me until now: but when the time came to separate the dishes made fiery by curry powder or other ingredients, I was hard put to devise a title for each section. Curry presented no problem, but what of the other recipes? I harked back to my scholarly(?) days and remembered the coal scuttles. Hence we have "noncurries." This is not to divide the world into curries and noncurries, only two sections of a cookbook—a modest goal.

Noncurries derive their fire from garlic; fresh or dried chili peppers; whole, cracked, and ground peppers from Sarawak, Indonesia, the Guianas, and Indochina; ginger; mustard; and horseradish.

Oysters en Cocotte

SERVES 6

"Cocotte" has several meanings, two of which have to do with heat in one form or another. These cocottes derive heat from two sources: the condiments used to "fire" the oysters and the heat from an oven. For another use of the word in a fiery context, consult your French lexicon.

These oysters are really fiery-warm rather than fiery-hot, and will make either a fish course at an elaborate meal or a main dish at a less pretentious gathering. The oysters must be fresh and preferably large, the size called "counts" in American grading.

2 quarts large oysters	*1½ teaspoons ground*
4 tablespoons butter	*coriander*
2 tablespoons flour	*1½ teaspoons ground*
1 teaspoon salt	*cumin*
1½ teaspoons curry	*1 tablespoon minced*
powder	*chives*
1½ teaspoons ground	*6 lemon wedges*
cardamom	

Preheat the oven to 250 degrees.

Poach oysters in their own liquor over a low flame. While they cook, melt the butter in a small saucepan over low heat. Meanwhile in a small bowl mix the flour, salt, curry powder, cardamom, coriander, and cumin. Put into butter and make a kind of loose paste, stirring until it is well cooked, about 5 minutes. To the saucepan gradually add liquor from the oysters until you have a thickish sauce. Put in the chives. When oysters are plump and done, distribute them among 6 cocottes and cover with sauce. Place cocottes in the slow oven and let them heat through. Put cocottes on warm plates, garnish with lemon wedges, and serve very hot.

If you are using this dish as a first course at a dinner, you could do worse than give your guests an imported Chablis, well chilled. If you plan to use it as a main course at supper, I suggest either the same Chablis, or a good cold beer. Toast triangles go well with the oysters.

Oysters Firepatrick

SERVES 4

This recipe is a fired up version of what the Japanese call oysters Kirkpatrick. The Maytoya oyster used for this dish in Japan is of medium size but succulent. I suggest you use the grade known as "select" in this country. I found no difficulty in eating a dozen oysters Kirkpatrick as a first course and frequently ate two dozen followed by a thin soup called dashi no-moto for my lunch. You will have no trouble eating twelve at lunch, or as a first course at dinner.

The recipe includes mirin, first cousin to sake, and used almost exclusively for cooking. It is available at any Japanese grocery or specialty shop.

1½ cups tomato ketchup	2½ tablespoons lemon
1 cup prepared hot	juice
horseradish	4½ tablespoons mirin
2½ tablespoons Tabasco	48 oysters on their shells

Place all ingredients except oysters in a bowl and mix well. Generously cover each freshly opened oyster on its own shell with the mixture, and place the oysters on a bed of rock salt. Put them under medium broiler heat for about 3 minutes, or until plump. Serve at once with small, triangular, thin sandwiches made with unsalted butter and brown bread. If you wish alcohol with this dish, let it be hot sake in small cups. Homemade coleslaw would complement the oysters.

Champagned Oysters

SERVES 4

Among the illusions of my youth were that oysters were aphrodisiac, champagne reduced inhibitions, and fiery food induced uncontrollable passion. If, I thought, I could but find a dish combining all three, the world, at least an important segment of it, would be my oyster. By the time I had learned enough about cooking to devise this triad, I had learned pragmatically that oysters are not aphrodisiac, champagne is less uninhibiting than whiskey or rum, and that fiery food in quantity was more likely to induce heartburn than passion. But I also learned that the recipe I finally evolved made for mighty fine eating. Here it is.

32 large oysters	Freshly ground black
16 slices prosciutto	pepper
1 bottle champagne, brut	4 parsley sprigs
1½ teaspoons Tabasco	

Preheat the oven to 250 degrees.

Remove oysters from liquor and drain by placing them between dish towels and patting from time to time. While oysters drain, cut ham slices in half. Pour champagne into a heavy, deep skillet, add Tabasco and bring to a simmer. Add drained oysters. Cover, and poach until oysters are plump and the edges curl. Remove oysters with a slotted spoon, and dry again between towels. Keep champagne warm in skillet. When the oysters have cooled sufficiently, spread the ham slices on a cutting board and place an oyster in the center of each slice. Gently grind a bit of black pepper over each oyster and roll the prosciutto around the oyster. Place the rolls in a shallow baking dish. Add 1 cup of the warm champagne to prevent drying. Put dish in the oven to heat through. When the oyster and ham rolls are ready, remove them and gracefully arrange 8 rolls per person on hot plates. Garnish with parsley and serve at once.

Serve with the dish very hot, thin buttered slices of melba toast. A green vegetable is unnecessary if you have a salad. The wine should be more of the same champagne, but chilled.

Crab Thermidor

SERVES 4

This dish is a fiery variation of the famous French recipe for lobster thermidor, in which I use already cooked and frozen Alaskan crab rather than fresh live lobster. Allow crab to thaw completely before starting to prepare the dish. In small quantities crab thermidor makes an excellent fish course for a formal meal; in larger quantities the recipe provides an equally good and fiery main dish.

5 large fresh mushrooms	*1½ cups clam juice*
6 tablespoons butter	*½ cup dry white wine*
1½ tablespoons flour	*¼ cup milk*
3 tablespoons dry mustard	*3 ten-ounce packages frozen Alaskan crabmeat*
½ tablespoon salt	
1 teaspoon freshly ground white pepper	*2 tablespoons grated parmesan cheese*
1 teaspoon Tabasco	

Wash mushrooms, and slice thin or cut into coarse pieces, including the stems. Melt 2 tablespoons butter in a small skillet and cook mushrooms until brown on all sides, but not limp. Drain. Discard any liquid and set aside. While mushrooms cook, mix in a bowl the flour, dry mustard, salt, and pepper. Place 3 tablespoons butter in a saucepan, melt, and add contents of bowl to make a paste. Add to it the Tabasco, clam juice, wine, and milk. Stir contents of the saucepan frequently over low heat to make a thick sauce. When sauce is cooked, add to it the mushrooms, and thawed crab. Stir all together well. Use remaining butter to grease 4 cocottes or gratin pans. Fill with the mixture from the saucepan and sprinkle well with the parmesan cheese. Place under a hot broiler for about 5 minutes or until the top is browned. Serve forthwith.

This recipe makes a comparatively mild, to my taste, thermidor. You can add fire by adding more Tabasco or more white pepper. I would not decrease the flour for additional mustard. By no means increase the salt ration. Serve with it hot buttered crusty rolls. The wine should be from the Moselle, and well chilled.

Fiery Crab Crêpes
SERVES 6

Unless you have access to a supply of fresh, not frozen, backfin lump meat of the blue crab, do not attempt this dish. The crab's habitat is the Atlantic Ocean and the Gulf of Mexico. The meat is very delicate in both taste and texture, both of which are destroyed by freezing. Because the taste is so delicate, I had doubts as to "firing" it up. I found by experiment however that this recipe did not overwhelm the taste.

Recipes for making the unsweetened French crêpes abound in good basic cookbooks and those on French cookery. The crêpes can be made as much as two weeks ahead of time and frozen against the hour of need. They should be allowed to thaw about 30 minutes before you proceed with the final preparation and cooking.

6 tablespoons butter
5 tablespoons sifted flour
1 pint clam juice
1 cup milk
¾ cup dry sherry
1 teaspoon cayenne
1½ teaspoons salt
2 teaspoons freshly
ground black pepper

1 teaspoon ground cumin
½ teaspoon ground ginger
1½ pounds backfin crab
lump, at room
temperature
18 crêpes

Place a flat baking pan large enough to hold 18 rolled crêpes over a pilot light or other very low heat until it is warm. Grease it lightly on the bottom and sides with 1 tablespoon or less of butter. Melt remaining butter in a large, heavy saucepan. Add flour and make a roux, stirring sufficiently to prevent browning. Heat clam juice slowly in another smaller saucepan. When roux is done, about 3 minutes, pour in the clam juice slowly, stirring the while. Add milk and sherry; cook until sauce begins to thicken. Put in cayenne, salt, black pepper, cumin, and ginger. Continue to heat sauce, stirring constantly. Just before the sauce begins to bead on the edges, taste and adjust the seasoning. When sauce is cooked put in the crab and mix gently into the sauce. Remove saucepan from heat.

Preheat the oven to 350 degrees.

Into the center of each crêpe place a tablespoon of the crab mixture. Roll the crêpe around it and fold in the ends. Place the rolled filled crêpe in the buttered baking dish, and continue the process until all crêpes have been used. Cover them with the remaining crab mixture and place the baking pan in the preheated oven until crêpes are thoroughly hot, about 20 minutes. Serve 2 of the crêpes on hot plates to each diner. Turn off oven and put remaining crêpes in it to keep warm for seconds.

Skinned, sliced tomatoes, garnished with fresh, minced dill or chives always receive an enthusiastic response. If you want wine I suggest a well-chilled brace of bottles from the Rheingau. A ripe melon served in the Spanish manner (cut into bite-size cubes and served on the rind) with lime wedges and a pepper grinder handy, makes an excellent end to the meal.

Gambas Piri Piri

SERVES 4

I found this blazing hot shrimp dish several years ago at a famous Madrid restaurant, El Antiquario. The recipe is one of the few cadged from restaurants with which I found it unnecessary to tamper to get the required fire. I ate the dish among the poshest surroundings; wherever you eat it you will find it equally good and equally hot. Gambas Piri Piri has the additional merit of being one of the simplest of fiery foods to prepare. I can wholeheartedly commend it.

2 lemons	3 dried red chili peppers
48 raw medium shrimp	Salt
¾ cup olive oil	4 half-inch wide strips
4 garlic cloves	pimento

Preheat the oven to 500 degrees.

Fill a large saucepan half full of water. Cut lemons in half. Squeeze half the juice into the water, add lemons and bring water to a boil. Toss in shrimp and boil them until half done, about 3 minutes. Drain shrimp, discarding lemons and water, and let cool. When they are cool enough to handle, remove shells and discard. Place 12 shrimp in each of 4 cocottes; pour over each dozen 3 tablespoons of olive oil. Peel garlic and cut lengthwise into 3 or 4 thick slivers. Divide among the cocottes. Cut the peppers into ½-inch pieces and distribute them in the oil around the shrimp. Sprinkle about ¼ teaspoon of salt over each cocotte and place them, uncovered, in the hot oven until oil begins to bubble, 5 or 6 minutes. Garnish with pimento strips and serve very hot.

Gambas Piri Piri are highly versatile. By reducing the ingredients by half, you have an unusual and splendid first course for a dinner. As the recipe stands you have a main dish and need only a salad and bread to complete a meal. Serve with it fresh crusty Spanish bread or its equivalent, and a salad of baby artichoke hearts and cherry tomatoes on a light foundation of chicory. The bread has two purposes: it is used to soak up the sauce, and acts as a fire extinguisher against the blaze the chili peppers ignite in your mouth and throat.

The dish is a fiery one, and no delicate wine will survive it. Despite the theory that white wine should always accompany fish or seafood, now is the time to forget theory and become realistic. What you need is a dry and rather rough red wine. A *vino corriente* from Spain, or a mountain red from California would be admirable.

Besugo al Forno

SERVES 4

During my journey through Spain when I found the delicious shrimp of the preceding recipe, I also found this unusual and fiery fish dish. Fish is usually bland but this recipe, which I had from a fishwife in a little village on the Atlantic coast just south of Vigo, deserves inclusion in this book because it was as inherently hot as it was delicious. The village had neither hotel nor restaurant, but the usual kindly Spaniard told us that one local fisherman's wife was a fine cook and for a few pesetas might cook us lunch. She did. We ate it in the kitchen off a deal table but it was fine fare as any we ever had in the grand restaurants of Madrid.

Besugo is a kind of sea bream; but you can substitute red snapper, as I discovered during the testing. The recipe takes time but the time is well spent. Buy a fish which weighs about four pounds after the head is removed. Have your fishmonger clean the fish, but not fillet it. The bones add to the flavor. Preparation of the dish is simplified if you start by chopping some of the ingredients.

3 lemons	2 teaspoons dry mustard
1 four-pound red snapper	2 medium dried red chili
4 tablespoons olive oil	peppers
2 tablespoons minced	2 large garlic cloves
parsley	¾ teaspoon salt
1 tablespoon cracked red	¼ teaspoon cayenne
pepper	

Preheat the oven to 350 degrees.

Quarter 2 lemons lengthwise and set aside for garnish. Cut the other lemon in half and then cut the halves into thin slices. Reserve. Place fish in a shallow baking dish greased with 1 tablespoon olive oil. With a sharp knife, slash fish to the backbone in 3 places. In each cut put a sprinkle of minced parsley, a lemon slice, ½ teaspoon cracked red pepper, and ½ teaspoon olive oil. Arrange remaining lemon slices across top of fish and sprinkle with remaining parsley. Place pan in the preheated oven and bake for about 40 minutes, depending on the thickness of the fish.

While fish cooks, warm rest of olive oil in a small skillet. Stir in mustard. Cut red chili peppers into 6 pieces. Peel garlic and cut into 6 pieces. Put chili peppers, garlic, and salt in oil. Raise heat to a low simmer, but do not allow oil to boil. When fish is flaky and done, remove from oven and transfer to a wooden cutting board. Using a sharp, broad-bladed knife, cut off tail and make an incision along the back of the fish. Scrape out the small bone. Using the same knife, split the fish. Remove backbone and cut the fillets in half.

Place them on a very hot platter. Remove chili peppers and garlic from oil in skillet and divide oil by pouring a quarter of it over each half fillet. Sprinkle the fillets lightly with cayenne. Garnish platter with lemon wedges and serve while still hot.

If you can get the little green peppers of Padron, cook them in olive oil and serve as a vegetable. Failing them, use thinly sliced eggplant, cooked in oil with tomato sauce. Hot Spanish bread makes an ideal starch with the fish. The wine should be Spanish. Miño Valley white wine, chilled, is both dry and gladdening. Rather than either a salad or a dessert, serve bowls of fruit and nuts.

Enchiladas con Pollo

SERVES 4 OR 6

A versatile dish is the enchilada. It can be made with diced fowl or ground meat, usually beef. It may be served alone as the main course. It can be part of a Mexican dinner. If the menu included Chili con Carne (page 125) the enchiladas should be stuffed with fowl. If you have arroz con pollo or chicken mole, the enchiladas should contain meat. Enchiladas are never served in the singular. To offer a guest one enchilada is like throwing a handful of mesquite twigs to a drowning man. You always offer at least two to a customer; sometimes as many as four.

Mexican tortillas are made by combining maize flour with water. The dough is shaped by hand into a round, very thin cake about five inches in diameter. Any good Mexican or general cookbook will give adequate instructions for making tortillas. They can also be bought frozen or canned. These tortillas serve admirably. Whether you make the little pancakes or buy them, they will be raw, hard, and brittle. They must be cooked and thus made soft and malleable. To cook tortillas for enchiladas, place ¼ cup cooking oil in a heavy skillet somewhat larger than the pancakes. When the oil is hot but not smoking put in tortillas one at a time. Let each cook for 2 seconds; turn it once, cook another 2 seconds, and immediately plunge into a bowl of ice water. Place on towels to dry. The tortillas are now soft enough to roll without breaking. Make sauce first and let stand a bit before you top the enchiladas.

8 ripe tomatoes
2 medium onions
2 garlic cloves
Vegetable oil
8 small hot green chili
  peppers
½ teaspoon dried oregano
Salt
Freshly ground black
  pepper

Tomato paste (optional)
2 cups diced cooked
  chicken
¼ pound sharp cheese
1 cup sour cream
½ teaspoon cayenne
14 tortillas, cooked and
  drained as above

Peel tomatoes, and chop them coarsely. Peel and chop onions. Peel and mince garlic. Heat 2 tablespoons oil in a heavy skillet, add onions and garlic and cook slowly until onions are soft but not brown. Put in tomatoes and cook over medium heat, mashing and stirring occasionally. While tomatoes cook, slice the chili peppers small, add them and the oregano to the skillet. After contents of skillet have become a kind of liquid mush, taste and add salt and pepper to bring out the flavor. Continue to simmer uncovered for about 20 minutes to reduce liquid in skillet, and make a thickish sauce. (If sauce is too thin, add tomato paste to thicken, and continue to simmer.)

Preheat the oven to 350 degrees.

While contents of skillet simmer, place chicken into a bowl, grate the cheese over it, and add the sour cream, a teaspoon of salt, and the cayenne. Mix well with a fork until contents of bowl are completely integrated. Taste and add more salt or cayenne as needed. Lightly grease a flat, oblong baking pan with a little vegetable oil. Be sure oil covers bottom and sides of pan. Place about a tablespoon of the chicken mixture from the bowl in the center of each tortilla and fold the tortilla over the mixture. Place the enchiladas, which is what you now have, close together in the greased pan. Spread the sauce over them, and bake in the preheated oven for 15 to 20 minutes, or until hot through. Serve forthwith.

A salad of well-washed Bibb lettuce or chicory with small chunks of avocado and a French dressing will take some of the fire out of the enchiladas, and will also complement them pleasantly. Mexican beer is an appropriate drink with the dish.

Chettle Deviled Chicken

SERVES 4

I spent a month with the Chettles on a P & O liner between Yoko-
hama and Port Everglades. Mrs. Chettle produced this recipe for
deviled chicken immediately when I said I was writing *Hellfire
Cookbook*. She and her family do come from Surrey, a county
which was the hotbed of witchcraft in the seventeenth century. And
she did say it was an old family dish not infrequently served on
Walpurgis Nacht, All Hallows' Eve, and the last night of the year.
Despite the foregoing, I do not think the recipe's origin is infernal.

Have your poulterer supply you with 4 chicken legs, thighs attached. I prefer chicken breast, but in this case the dark meat adds
flavor.

½ pound (2 sticks) butter	*1 tablespoon salt*
1 tablespoon cracked red pepper	*¼ cup dry English mustard*
1 tablespoon cracked black pepper	*4 chicken legs*

Place butter in a low-sided pie pan, and melt over low heat. While
butter melts, make the "devil pepper": mix the peppers and salt in a
small bowl until they are indistinguishable from one another.
Spread the mustard on a sheet of wax paper, and cover with another
sheet. Using a beer bottle or rolling pin, crush mustard until no
lumps remain. Remove the top layer of wax paper. By now the
butter should have melted. With a sharp knife, slash the chicken to
the bone on one side, making 4 cuts. Dip each piece of chicken in
the melted butter and dredge both sides in mustard. Sprinkle both
sides with devil pepper and put chicken in a shallow roasting pan.
Pour remaining butter around the chicken and place under moderate broiler heat for 10 minutes. Baste with butter in pan and turn.
Baste again. Return to broiler and broil another 10 minutes. Repeat
basting process. Raise heat and cook on one side for about 5 minutes
more. If that side has begun to brown, baste, and turn over. Baste
once more and cook another 5 minutes. The chicken will now be
done.

Chettle Deviled Chicken is a party dish. I suggest you precede it with an hors d'oeuvre or a thin soup. Chicken and rice have a natural affinity and rice should be your starch. Make a sauce for it by scraping the bottom of the broiler pan and adding a bit of flour along with a ½ teaspoon of dried marjoram for seasoning. When paste is cooked pour in enough chicken stock to make a fairly thick gravy. Remove to a hot serving platter, garnish with watercress, and serve. Any green vegetable goes well with the chicken. The wine should be white, and dry. Instead of a salad, follow the chicken with a bowl of fresh fruit, or a melon, cut into quarters and accompanied with lime wedges. Provide pepper grinders that each guest may season his own melon.

Sacrificial Fowl

SERVES 8

The priests of nearly all primitive religions propitiated or thanked their gods with human sacrifice. In many instances cannibalism was part of the ritual. As civilizations prosper, they become more effete, and their rituals more effete with them. Gradually fowl replaced people in the rites of thanksgiving and propitiation. It might well follow that the turkey at the first Thanksgiving was, albeit unwittingly, a kind of sacrificial offering in which the fowl stood surrogate to the man. Eating the offering after it was sacrificed was more common than unusual in the old rites. Whatever the facts, this recipe differs so markedly from normal roast turkey that I doubt it was a dish reserved for celebrating a special kind of thanksgiving. The recipe? It was found among the yellowed pages of a famous Salem witch-hunter. You should allow two days to prepare the dish. The time will not be wasted. The first day:

2 large carrots	*1 tablespoon salt*
2 large onions	*4 parsley sprigs*
2 large celery ribs with leaves	*1 ten-pound turkey, jointed*
12 peppercorns	

Scrape carrots, peel onions, wash celery, and chop each coarsely. Put them in a deep, large, heavy saucepan or soup kettle. Add remaining ingredients except turkey. Pour in 3 quarts of water. Cover pan and bring to a boil. Gradually add turkey pieces but keep water simmering. When all the turkey is in the pot, partially cover, and simmer until turkey is done, about 2 hours, skimming if necessary. When done remove turkey with a slotted spoon or a fork and refrigerate. Raise heat and simmer, uncovered, until stock has been reduced by half. Strain, discarding all solids. Place stock in a bowl and refrigerate.

On the second day, and about 3 hours before serving time, remove turkey from refrigerator; cut meat off bones, discarding them and all skin and membranes. Cut turkey meat into 1-inch cubes and place in top of double boiler. Heat slowly over water. Skim turkey fat from the bowl of stock, reserving fat and stock.

12 long, thin fresh green *chili peppers*	*6 tablespoons flour* *½ cup dry sherry*
2 teaspoons cracked red *chili peppers*	*½ cup milk* *16 slices prosciutto*

Split chili peppers. Remove seeds and membranes, discarding both. Chop peppers into ½-inch squares and set aside. Pour 1½ pints of the turkey stock into a saucepan, bring to a boil, and add green chili peppers and cracked red peppers. Cover saucepan and simmer gently. While contents of saucepan simmer, put 6 tablespoons of reserved turkey fat into another saucepan, melt, and add flour to make a roux. When roux is dark yellow and softish, gradually add hot stock with peppers, stirring the while to make a sauce. As sauce thickens, add sherry and milk. Stir until sauce comes almost to a boil, but do not let it boil. If sauce is too thick, thin with more stock; if too thin, thicken by making a paste with 2 tablespoons sauce and 2 of arrowroot, and stir into the sauce. By now the turkey cubes should be warmed through. Add them to the sauce, heat a few minutes and serve on slices of prosciutto.

A mixed green salad should accompany or follow the turkey. Hot rolls or rice would be good starches with the dish. Beer or a light red or white dry wine will not douse the fire but will slake the thirst. Any green vegetable will go well with the turkey.

Cabbages and Ducks

SERVES 6

For all its title this recipe was not conceived by either the Walrus or the Carpenter during their famous massacre of oysters on the Strand. Although the omnivorous pair mentioned cabbages casually they were too much concerned with luring oysters from their beds to give a thought to ducks. The dish really is an adaptation of one I had several years ago in Normandy where the ducks are almost as good as the oysters, and the cabbages are superb.

2 *five-pound ducks*	6 *green chili peppers*
1 *large carrot*	8 *garlic cloves*
1 *celery rib with leaves*	1 *piece fresh ginger, 2*
9 *medium onions*	*inches long by ¾ inch*
2 *parsley sprigs*	*wide, and ¼ inch thick*
12 *black peppercorns*	2 *tablespoons butter*
3 *teaspoons salt*	3 *tablespoons flour*
6 *large cabbage leaves*	½ *cup red wine vinegar*
1 *tablespoon turmeric*	

Joint the ducks. With a sharp knife, a boning knife is best, remove and discard all fat but reserve skin. (If you wish, the duck fat can be rendered and reserved for another use.) For the dish itself, use only the breasts, thighs, and legs. Make a stock with remainder of duck, including skin. To do this, cut carrot into 1-inch rounds, celery into 1-inch pieces, and quarter 1 onion. Place all in a 4-quart saucepan and add parsley, peppercorns, 1 teaspoon salt, and 6 cups water. Bring to a boil, put in remaining pieces of duck, and simmer for at least 1 hour to make a stock.

Meanwhile, back at the range, place the cabbage leaves in the bottom of another large saucepan or soup kettle. Put the edible duck pieces on the bed of cabbage. Mix remaining salt and the turmeric. Julienne the chili peppers, retaining half the seeds. Quarter remaining onions, and peel garlic. Peel ginger and thinly slice. Place all these ingredients on top of duck. Skim fat off duck stock, and pour 3 cups of stock over duck. Bring to a boil, cover, and simmer for 1 hour. Uncover, and continue to simmer until duck is done, about 15 minutes longer.

Melt butter in skillet, add flour to make a roux. Strain some of the liquid from duck kettle, discarding solids in stock, and add to roux to make a sauce, which should not be too thick, or yet too thin, but thinner than thicker. You can best thin it by using additional duck stock. Five minutes before you are ready to serve, add the vinegar to the duck. Stir well and allow simmering to continue. Remove duck pieces to warm plates, being sure none of the cabbage, onion slices, or peppers cling to the meat. Serve sauce separately.

The best vegetable with this dish is more cabbage which should be shredded and boiled briefly, until done but not mushy, and seasoned with salt and pepper only. It should cook about 5 minutes. For starch, I suggest buttered wide noodles. The sauce is intended for the duck, but will not harm the noodles. The wine, and here I can be specific, should be a claret: Château Maillard. It is inexpensive but "turns on" the wine bibber.

Chili con Carne

SERVES 6

In Mexico they call this dish *carne en salsa chili colorado*. The Texans borrowed the idea from the Mexicans, altered it a bit, and now claim it as their own. Technically this particular dish should be called *chili con carne con frijoles*, as it contains beans. I got the recipe from the late C. C. Shelton, a professional and peripatetic knife sharpener who once lived in west Texas. He was full of skill, good works, and fantastic stories, some of them true. On one of his periodic visits to sharpen my knives I told him that I wrote about food. He promised me his own recipe for chili con carne and duly provided it, insisting that it was originally Mexican and authentic in every detail. This I beg leave to doubt. No one, Mexican, Indian, Spaniard, or Texan, could eat the quantity of suet called for in his recipe. So having borrowed it, I changed it a bit and it is now mine own.

4 tablespoons cubed beef
 suet
2 pounds ground top
 round
1 teaspoon salt
1 tablespoon freshly
 ground black pepper
½ teaspoon oregano
½ teaspoon celery salt

½ teaspoon cayenne
5 teaspoons chili powder
2 teaspoons paprika
2 teaspoons ground
 sesame seeds
1 tablespoon ground
 cumin
2 one-pound cans kidney
 beans

Render the suet in a skillet. With a slotted spoon remove and then discard all solid residue. To liquid suet in the skillet add: meat, salt, pepper, and other seasonings. Cook over a medium heat, stirring now and again, for 15 minutes. Drain beans, stir into skillet, heat through and serve.

Tostados, Mexican beer, and a simple Mexican cooked vegetable salad dressed with lime juice and vinegar are noteworthy accompaniments to this chili.

Apprentice Loose Beef

SERVES 2

Many years ago a young friend just entering the arcane world of cookery conceived this recipe. He was prompted by laziness, a strong urge to stay with an unexpected supper guest, and the mistaken belief that fiery food is conducive to the celebration of Aphrodite's rites. Unhappily, the dish failed to support that belief.

Besides its fire, the recipe has other merits. It is ridiculously easy to prepare. With skilled, uninterrupted application in the kitchen you can prepare and cook it in about twenty minutes. The ingredients are few and most will already be in your larder. This recipe is not exactly what my friend cooked the first time, but it is close enough.

3 scallions
3 long green chili peppers
2 small dried red chili
 peppers
1 generous tablespoon
 butter

¾ teaspoon salt
¾ pound very lean ground
 sirloin

Slice the scallions very thinly. Remove tops and bottoms of green peppers and slice peppers thinly. Mince the red peppers and discard about half the seeds. Place butter in large skillet over a moderate flame. When butter has melted, put in scallions and both peppers. Add salt. Mix well. Cook slowly, stirring often until contents of skillet are soft. Meanwhile break up ground beef into small chunks and add to skillet. From now on you have to slave over the hot stove wielding a 4-tined fork. With it break up meat as you turn it, to brown on all sides. How long you cook the meat depends on whether you like it well done, rare, or pink. You can tell by observation when it has reached the degree of doneness you like. Serve on hot plates. By using 1½ pounds of beef and doubling the other ingredients, you can make enough for 4 people.

Boiled parsleyed new potatoes make a good starchy vegetable with the beef, as they help absorb the fire. Plain boiled broccoli would be a welcome green vegetable. The wine should be a little rough.

Burmese Beef

SERVES 4

The real reason that Tommy Atkins wanted to return to Mandalay was not because a Burmese girl was waiting or that he liked the sound of temple bells. What he wanted was gingered Burmese beef which will lure a man to go anywhere or do anything, especially if he has been living on army rations.

The fiery taste of the beef depends on ginger. Fresh ginger is normally to be preferred to ground, but not in this dish. You should allow at least an hour, two hours would be better, for marination. Sometimes the recipe is made with onions, but they detract from the flavor of both the beef and the ginger. The meat should be lean sirloin and cut into strips 2 inches long, 1 inch wide, and ¼ inch thick.

2 tomatoes
1 teaspoon garlic salt
1 teaspoon chili powder
1 teaspoon turmeric
2½ tablespoons ground
* ginger*

2 pounds sirloin, cut as
* above*
2 tablespoons butter
4 parsley sprigs

Skin tomatoes and cut into small pieces. Place in a large bowl. Add garlic salt, chili powder, turmeric, and ginger. Stir well. Put in slices of beef and mix thoroughly, coating the beef well. Cover and marinate at least 1 hour. At end of marination, heat butter in a large skillet and add contents of bowl. Coat well with butter, and simmer, uncovered, for about 30 minutes. Cooking longer will make the beef tough. Serve on hot plates, garnished with a parsley sprig each, and place before your guests at once.

This beef is both reasonably fiery and hearty. Against the fire I recommend pumpernickel. Have, too, a green vegetable or a bland green salad with an oil and vinegar dressing, allowing each diner to add salt and pepper as he chooses. Wine presents a bit of a problem. The Burmese produce none worthy of notice; my inclination is to go farther east and get from Japan a good sake, but serve it well chilled rather than warm.

Steak au Poivre Flambé

SERVES 4

A noted American gourmet, amateur chef, writer, and world-traveled food and restaurant critic—few have such culinary credentials—told mutual friends that he is inordinately fond of this dish. Apparently he uses it as a kind of test of a restaurant's place in the gastronomic scheme of things. In unpretentious eateries the dish is listed simply and honestly as Pepper Steak. It may or may not be flamed. In ostentatious dining places, especially those calling themselves "Steak Houses" it is called Steak Au Poivre and is invariably flamed. Often the blaze is so flamboyant that you expect it to scorch the ceiling. Call it what you will, the propriety of including this dish here is beyond cavil. Fiery it is and flaming it is. Hell may have no fury like a woman scorned, I wouldn't know. I do know that Hell hath no other dish more in keeping with the locale.

The following recipe is based on the assumption that you have two large skillets: one for the cooking, the other for flaming. You can substitute plain salt for kosher salt, but the latter is coarser and makes for happier steaks.

2 tablespoons cracked
  black pepper
1 teaspoon cracked red
  pepper
4 Delmonico steaks, about
  6 ounces each
4 tablespoons kosher salt

2 tablespoons butter
½ teaspoon Tabasco
1 tablespoon Worchester-
  shire sauce
4 tablespoons cognac
3 tablespoons minced
  chives

Thoroughly mix the cracked peppers in a small bowl. Remove almost all fat from the steaks. Place them on a sheet of wax paper
spread on a smooth, firm surface. Sprinkle a teaspoon of the mixed
peppers on top of each steak. Press the peppers well into the meat
with the heel of your hand. Turn steaks over and repeat the pepper-
ing process. The beef must rest at least 30 minutes after such brutal
treatment. Go away and prepare other parts of the meal, or read a
book, or have a drink. You can combine the drink with either of the
suggestions, but do not further touch the steaks until you are ready
to cook them.

Cover the bottom of one skillet with salt, and smooth it to make
an even and level layer. Place the skillet over high heat until all
water has evaporated and salt is completely dry. Meanwhile, a matter of less than a minute, put the other skillet over moderate flame.
Place the steaks on the salt and cook for 15 seconds over high heat.
Turn steaks on the salt and cook 30 seconds. These times will produce a very rare steak. If you want your meat pink or well done,
reduce fire under the skillet and continue to cook until the meat is
done to your taste. Do not turn the steaks again. Remove steaks
from their bed of salt, place them in the second, and by now hot
skillet. Divide the butter into 4 parts and place a gobbet on each
steak. Dash in the Tabasco, sprinkle in the Worcestershire. Reduce
heat slightly and pour in the cognac. Ignite it. With a long-handled
spoon baste the steaks with the flaming liquid. Remove to a hot
platter. Stir the pan juices well and pour over the steaks. Sprinkle
them with chives and serve immediately. The flaming ritual can take
place at the table by putting the steaks into a hot blazer pan of a
chafing dish and then adding the 2 sauces and cognac. Blaze and proceed as above.

For fire-fighting purposes serve the steaks on buttered toast
rounds. Any green vegetable or macedoine of vegetables goes well

with the steaks. A good red Burgundy, I like a Montrachet, is excellent with the meat.

"Perhaps" Lamb Chops

SERVES 4

You receive this Indonesian recipe at fifth hand. The dish was first cooked for me by a good but, alas, not intimate friend. She in turn had it from a Dutchman long resident in Java. He said he got it from a highly skilled Javanese dancer, apparently more than a pas-de-deux acquaintance. She was known as "Perhaps" Banjuwangi because perhaps she would and perhaps she wouldn't. She, in turn, wiled the recipe from a chef in Bali where women dance as men "fought in Nelson's fleet; stripped to the waist and bare to the feet." With these antecedents the dish should be appetizing in many respects. It is. It also takes five hours to marinate the chops.

1 small onion	*¼ cup white wine vinegar*
⅓ cup minced celery	*4 teaspoons A-1 sauce*
3 garlic cloves	*1 teaspoon cayenne*
2 tablespoons olive oil	*¾ cup prepared mustard*
1 tablespoon ground cardamom	*2 bay leaves*
½ tablespoon ground coriander	*Zest and juice of 1 lemon*
½ tablespoon ground cumin	*Zest and juice of ½ lime*
	8 double lamb chops, "Frenched"

Peel and mince onion. Place in a bowl with the celery and set aside. Peel garlic, put through a press, and add to bowl. Put oil in a saucepan over low heat. Bring oil to a simmer, add contents of bowl, raise heat to moderate, and cook until onion is soft. Add the 3 spices, lower heat, and simmer 2 to 3 minutes. Remove from heat. Stir in vinegar, A-1 sauce, cayenne, and mustard. Add bay leaves. Mince lemon and lime zest. Squeeze juice from fruits. Place zest and juice in saucepan. Stir contents of pan well. Place over low heat and simmer for 5 minutes. Remove from heat and allow to cool. Arrange lamb chops in a single layer in a shallow baking pan. Pour contents of saucepan over chops to cover completely and marinate for 5 hours, turning the chops at least twice.

Preheat the oven to 400 degrees. Cover pan with aluminum foil and place in the preheated oven for 20 minutes. Remove pan from oven, turn chops, baste, re-cover pan, and return to oven for another 20 minutes. Chops should be done, but another 5 minutes will not damage them. The marinade will also have become thinner. Serve chops on a hot platter or hot plates. Pour marinade into a silver gravy boat and serve separately as sauce.

The chops scream for rice. My friend served a red Burgundy with the main course which she preceded with a rare Chinese egg drop soup. French-cut green beans would be a good vegetable. Whatever you serve before, with, or after them, the chops are delicious.

Callos à la Madrileño

SERVES 6

As I have noted now and again, Spanish dishes are regional rather than national. Hence Spanish recipes are variable and versatile. An example is this method of cooking tripe as it is prepared in Madrid. You can be sure that a dozen different Spanish cookbooks would give you at least a dozen ways of cooking Callos à la Madrileño. This recipe is similar to but different from any of the others. The difference lies in what this particular cook whose name, appropriately, is Carmen, added to and subtracted from other recipes. Carmen's version has been adapted to available American ingredients by her erstwhile employer, who is also a magnificent and imaginative cook.

To cook the tripe to the best advantage you should allow three days. It can be done in two, but the extra 24 hours improves the flavor by allowing the ingredients to become better acquainted with one another.

3 pounds honeycomb
tripe
½ cup kosher salt
¼ cup lemon juice
4 tablespoons white wine
vinegar
1 large carrot
2 medium Spanish onions
¼ cup dry sherry
¼ cup dry vermouth
4 garlic cloves
12 black peppercorns
1 teaspoon cracked red
pepper
1 bay leaf

1 teaspoon dried thyme
1½ pounds veal shin bone,
with some meat
attached
Salt
4 ounces chorizo
(sausage)
1 slice baked ham, 1-inch
thick
1 large fresh red chili
pepper
2 tablespoons tomtato
paste
Cayenne, if needed

With a stiff brush, scrub the tripe well. Wash it in several waters, and scrub again. Rub kosher salt and lemon juice into it with the heel of your hand. Place in a bowl, cover with fresh water and add vinegar. Let stand for 30 minutes. Remove tripe, discarding water. Wash tripe again to remove all salt and lemon juice. Place tripe in a saucepan, barely cover with fresh water, cover saucepan, and boil 15 minutes. Drain.

While tripe is boiling, scrape carrot and slice moderately thin. Peel and mince 1 onion. Put carrot and onion in a small bowl and add the sherry and vermouth. Peel and mash garlic, add to bowl. Place the whole peppercorns, the cracked red pepper, the bay leaf, and the thyme on a square of cheesecloth, and tie to make a bouquet garni. Drain tripe and place in a larger saucepan. Add contents of bowl, the bouquet garni, and veal bone. Pour in enough fresh water to cover contents of saucepan. Cover and simmer for 2 to 3 hours until veal is falling from bone and tripe is tender. Drain contents of saucepan into a bowl, reserving the liquid. Remove and discard shin bone. Cut veal into small cubes, and tripe into 2-inch squares. Taste liquid and add salt if needed. Put liquid and meat in separate bowls. Refrigerate overnight.

Next day skim all fat from liquid and discard. Remove tripe and veal from refrigerator and bring to room temperature. Peel another onion and slice very thinly. Set aside. Cut chorizo into ¼-inch slices, and cube ham to make 1½ cups. Cut red chili pepper in half. Place reserved liquid in an ovenproof pottery casserole, add tripe, veal, onion slices, ham, chili pepper, and tomato paste. With a wooden spoon, stir contents of casserole until well mixed. Now you face a decision. You can return casserole to refrigerator and allow mixture to spend another night, or you can continue the cooking and serve the dish in about an hour. If you elect to wait, remove casserole from refrigerator about 2 hours before you plan to dine, and bring it to room temperature. In either case you proceed as follows.

Preheat the oven to 450 degrees.

Place casserole, uncovered, over low heat and simmer to reduce liquid until you have a thickish broth. Remove chili pepper, and taste liquid in casserole. If the dish is not so fiery as you wish, add cayenne. Cover casserole and place in the preheated oven until it begins to bubble. The tripe is now ready to serve. To do that in traditional manner you divide the contents of the casserole among 6, hot, individual pottery bowls. Serve with the tripe, and this is important, a laudable quantity of sliced, hard-crusted Spanish or French bread. Eat the meat with a fork and sop up the sauce with the bread.

With the tripe serve only a mixed salad, using seasonal lettuces, a cucumber, and a tomato or two. I suggest a dressing of one part lemon juice, three parts olive oil, salt, and freshly ground pepper. A couple of bottles of good red Spanish wine—and there are good red Spanish wines—should be offered with the tripe.

Veal Vaquero

SERVES 4

A *vaquero* is a Mexican cowboy. In the old days he drove cattle to market as American cowboys drove cattle to the railhead. Whether Mexican or American, their "cookie" fed them on the trail with either slumgullion or beans, and sometimes a side of bacon. Occasionally and if the drive had been good, the trail boss would give his vaqueros or cowhands a special meal the night before the end of the trail. He allowed them to slaughter a dogie, and if the cook were a Mexican, as he not infrequently was, he would make a special sauce for the veal. The recipe below is refined somewhat from that cooked on the lone prairie, as it is cooked on the range at home. Have your butcher cut the veal about ¼-inch thick. Two and a half pounds of meat may seem a lot for four people, but after you have removed the bone, fat, and sinew, and cut the meat into the proper shape, you will not have too much. Make the sauce first that it may age, rest, and gather strength.

18 fresh red chili peppers	1 teaspoon ground
5 large garlic cloves	juniper berries
2½ tablespoons tequila	Vegetable oil
1 teaspoon lemon juice	2½ pounds veal cutlet,
1½ teaspoons salt	¼-inch thick
1 teaspoon ground	
coriander	

Split the chili peppers. Remove and discard the seeds. Peel the garlic. Place chili peppers, garlic, and all other ingredients down to but not including the vegetable oil, in a blender. Add 3 tablespoons oil and blend at moderate speed for about 3 minutes. With a narrow rubber spatula push all the particles which have stuck to the side of the blender to the bottom. Pour the sauce into a wide shallow bowl and set aside while you prepare the veal.

Preheat the oven to 375 degrees.

With a very sharp boning knife, remove the bone from each cutlet, and trim off all the fat around the edges. Cover each slice of veal with a dish towel, and pound the meat with a wooden mallet until it is no more than ⅛-inch thick. Cut pieces about 4-inches long, removing and discarding interior fat and sinew as you cut. You should have at least 8 such slices. Spread each piece lightly with the sauce, using a pastry brush. Roll the veal with the spread side inside. Fasten each roll with a toothpick to maintain its shape. Place about 1 tablespoon of vegetable oil in a flat baking pan, grease bottom and sides well and arrange the veal rolls, gently touching, in the bottom of the pan. Spread a modicum of the sauce over each roll. Place the pan in the preheated oven and cook for about 40 minutes or until the veal is done through. Meanwhile, place the remaining sauce in a small saucepan and warm over a low flame. When ready to serve the veal, place the sauce in a gravy boat or small silver bowl. Give each customer at least 2 veal rolls and pass the hot sauce for those who do not think the meat has sufficient fire. Advise your guests to taste the veal before adding more sauce.

The vaquero, of course, drank tequila or pulque before, with, and after the meal. I do not recommend either tequila or pulque with

Veal Vaquero. Mexican beer is excellent, but so are many California red wines. Take your choice. Hot, hard, crusty bread with butter, and *colache*, a Mexican succotash made with squash, maize, and tomatoes, goes well with the veal. Forget about a salad, unless you are salad-prone.

Nonbarbequed Barbequed Spareribs

SERVES 4

Although I am opposed on principle to cookouts and barbeques, I do not wish to be churlish and withhold a recipe which many ardent barbequers may find edifying. The recipe has an advantage over most similar dishes in that it can be cooked outside on the terrace or inside in the kitchen. Thus it is available to the barbeque cook all year and he need not abstain from his smoldering art during the frigid months. Another advantage of this recipe redounds to the cook's wife. Clinical tests have shown that among the households tested, well over 90 percent of barbeque cooks are men and that wives, acting as scullery maids, clean up after their husbands. If the dish is cooked in the kitchen the clearing and cleaning is much simplified. Dirty implements and dishes need be carried only across the room to the dishwasher instead of across the terrace through part of the house to the scullery. Wherever you prepare this dish, you will find that the spareribs are in the best tradition of the barbeque. I give below the "cook-in" version. The barbequer can easily convert the recipe to a cookout version. In any case allow seven or eight hours for marination and cooking.

2 onions
6 garlic cloves
2 tablespoons chili powder
2 tablespoons dry mustard
2 teaspoons ground coriander
2 teaspoons ground cumin
1 teaspoon cayenne

2 teaspoons sugar
4 tablespoons Worcestershire sauce
¾ cup bourbon
1¼ cups tomato ketchup
½ cup cider vinegar
2 tablespoons fresh lemon juice
2 two-pound slabs baby pork spareribs

Peel onions and garlic. Chop both coarsely and mix in a bowl. Set aside. In another larger bowl place all the dry ingredients and mix them thoroughly. Add to the same bowl, one at a time, the liquid ingredients, stirring each one into the mixture before adding the next. This will give you a smooth, moderately liquid paste. Add onions and garlic to the bowl and amalgamate them with the other contents. Remove as much fat as possible from the spareribs. Using a pastry brush, paint both sides and the edges of each slab and let spareribs marinate a minimum of 6 hours; overnight would be better. About 3 hours before you intend to serve the spareribs, remove all the marinade paste. A rubber spatula will be helpful for this process. Place marinade in a saucepan and cover.

Preheat the oven to 350 degrees.

Cut the spareribs into sections of 5 ribs each and place them in one or two baking pans. Into each pan pour ½ cup of water. Place the pans, uncovered, in the preheated oven and cook for 1 hour. Check water level in pans: they should not be allowed to dry out. Add more water if required and cook another hour. Check water level again. Cook 30 minutes more and remove from oven. Drain; the water will have picked up the excess fat. The spareribs are now ready. After the second water-level check, place the saucepan with the marinade over very low heat so that it will be thoroughly hot but not boiling when the meat is done. Serve marinade separately.

A green vegetable should be part of the meal. For starch offer thick-crusted, hot bread on the side. You will find that spreading a little of the sauce on the bread will enhance the taste of each. I leave the choice of a wine to you, but beer would be better.

Tongue of The Shrew

SERVES 4

This recipe was brought to me by a friend who had just returned from one of her many cruises in the Aegean. She had been aboard *The Shrew*, a ninety-foot ketch out of Valletta, with a Maltese crew and a Greek chef named Omega Zypheros. He was a very old man and a wine bibber, but cooked fiery food divinely. Hence this tongue.

1 medium onion
4 whole cloves
1 medium carrot
1 celery rib with leaves
2 bay leaves
1 teaspoon cumin seed
4 whole juniper berries
8 whole black
   peppercorns
1 four-pound smoked
   beef tongue
6 garlic cloves
2 tablespoons freshly
   grated lemon peel

½ teaspoon ground
   cinnamon
1½ teaspoons freshly
   ground black pepper
1½ teaspoons freshly
   grated horseradish
2 teaspoons prepared
   mustard
½ teaspoon cayenne
½ teaspoon Tabasco
¾ cup dry white wine
4 watercress sprigs

Peel the onion and stick the cloves in its sides; place in a saucepan big enough to hold the tongue without crowding. Scrape carrot and cut into ½-inch rounds. Cut the celery into 1-inch squares and chop the leaves coarsely. Snuggle the carrot pieces and celery alongside the cloved onion. Toss in the bay leaves, and sprinkle in the cumin, juniper berries, and peppercorns. Place the tongue on top and cover it with water. Cover the saucepan, and place over moderately high flame until water comes to a boil. Reduce heat and simmer the tongue for about 3 hours, or until it is tender when punctured with a silver fork. Remove from fire and allow tongue to cool in the cooking liquid.

When cool enough to handle, remove tongue from saucepan, discard the gristle and bone at the thick end. With a small sharp knife slit the skin on the underneath side, being careful not to cut into the meat. Starting at the thick end, skin the tongue and discard the skin as well as the root section. Place the tongue on its side, and with a long, thin, very sharp slicer, cut slices on the bias a little less than ¼-inch thick. Allow 5 medium-length pieces per serving. Peel the garlic, put it through a press, and combine with the lemon peel. Put in all the remaining ingredients except watercress, and merge them completely. Preheat the oven to 375 degrees.

Arrange the tongue slices, overlapping as little as possible, in a wide casserole with a tight-fitting lid. Spread contents of bowl over tongue. Cover the casserole, place in the oven, and cook for 25 minutes. Check casserole to be sure liquid has not been totally absorbed. If it has, add another tablespoon or two of wine and cook another 5 minutes. By this time most of the liquid should have been absorbed by the meat and the tongue ready to be served. It should be moist but little if any liquid should remain. Remove tongue slices to hot individual plates, or to a hot platter, garnish with watercress and serve.

Boiled, peeled, baby new potatoes with maître d'hôtel butter complement the tongue. Brussels sprouts always go well with smoked meat of any kind and add to the adornment of the dish. Or, if you prefer, serve a green salad containing among other things, fresh raw Brussels sprouts, quartered. Red meat takes red wine. In theory it is a good adage but do not become a slave to it. The tongue was cooked in white wine: I suggest you serve the same, slightly chilled, with the meal.

VEGETABLES

Except for creamed spinach, artichokes, fresh white asparagus, and Brussels sprouts, I am not overly fond of vegetables. I find it a bit of a chore to cook and test vegetable recipes. Moreover, there are few fiery dishes using vegetables. Nevertheless, I have been able to find a round dozen—why not a square dozen, or a hexagonal dozen?—such dishes so that the vegetable lover will not be too badly shortchanged when he buys this book.

I hope that vegetable lovers who are, at the same time, partial to fiery food will find the following examples more than adequate to rate a section to themselves.

Lentils

SERVES 6

Lentils are part of the oldest known recipe. They were the main ingredient of the mess of potage with which Esau cozened his brother out of his birthright. Besides lentils this recipe calls for two fiery condiments—curry powder and coriander—as well as garlic and onions, smoldering if not fiery. The dish will not make you reach blindly, because of tear-filled eyes, for a cooling beer or a bit of bread, but you will know that you are eating no ordinary vegetable.

With ready-to-cook lentils allow about 1 hour for cooking.

2 medium onions	*1 large garlic clove*
3 cups chicken or veal stock	*1½ teaspoons curry powder*
1 teaspoon salt	*1 teaspoon ground coriander*
1 cup lentils	
3 tablespoons butter	

Peel and chop onions. Place stock in saucepan, add salt, lentils, and half the onion. Cover and bring to a boil. Reduce heat and simmer 40 minutes. Drain lentils. There will be very little liquid as most will have been absorbed. About 10 minutes before lentils are done, melt butter in a skillet, and add remaining onions. Smash or mince garlic and put in skillet. Cook over low heat until almost brown. Put in lentils, and sprinkle over them the curry powder and coriander. Mix well with a wooden spoon. Cover and cook slowly about 10 minutes. By then the lentils should be done and almost dry. Serve hot.

Braised Leeks

SERVES 4

Centuries before Moses was found hiding in the bulrushes, Egyptians were raising leeks for their feasts and ordinary meals. That they were highly esteemed is indicated by this recipe. It is said to have been found written on papyrus in the tomb of a high priest of Set, god of the underworld. Items buried with the pharaohs and other high officials were not casual things. Mostly they were intended to aid and comfort the deceased in his journey to the next world. It follows that the vegetable, or at least this recipe was rather special. I think it still is.

8 medium leeks	*1 teaspoon Tabasco*
1 teaspoon salt	*1 cup beef stock*
2 tablespoons butter	
2 teaspoons prepared mustard	

Cut off and discard the root end and most of the green part of the leeks. Strip off the outermost layer as you do with scallions. Wash leeks thoroughly and cut them into 2- or 3-inch lengths. Fill a 2-quart saucepan half full of water, put in salt, bring to a boil and add leeks. Cover and blanch leeks about 5 minutes. Drain and dry leeks between towels. Melt butter in a heavy skillet and add mustard and Tabasco. When mixture is hot, add leeks and sauté for about 5 minutes. Pour in stock, stir well to coat leeks and to mix stock with contents of skillet. Cover tightly, reduce heat, and simmer leeks for 45 minutes, or until tender. Drain and serve.

Smoldering Creamed Spinach

SERVES 4

Creamed spinach is usually the blandest of vegetables and is often prescribed for convalescents from stomach disorders. Not so this version. It is no raging conflagration, but smolders like the coals over which you toast marshmallows or pop corn. You will find it a pleasant and piquant change from other methods of preparation. The recipe makes modest servings for four. If you wish to be more bountiful, increase all ingredients by 50 percent.

1 medium onion	*¼ teaspoon cayenne*
1 tablespoon butter	*¾ cup milk*
2 tablespoons freshly	*1 ten-ounce package*
grated or powdered	*frozen chopped spinach*
horseradish	*2 slices prosciutto*
1 tablespoon dry mustard	*Nutmeg*

Peel and mince onion. Melt butter in a saucepan, add onion, and cook, stirring occasionally, until onion is almost translucent. Put in horseradish, mustard, and cayenne. Stir well and continue cooking until you have a kind of paste, approximately 3 minutes. Add milk, stirring well. When sauce begins to thicken, remove from heat, and force through a strainer. Reserve the liquid but discard solids remaining in strainer. Return sauce to pan and keep warm.

Cook spinach according to package directions. While spinach cooks, dice the prosciutto. When spinach is done place in the strainer and squeeze out all water. Sprinkle with the minced prosciutto and chop all again. Combine spinach with sauce, mix well, and heat thoroughly. Sprinkle with grated nutmeg just before serving, but no croutons, please.

Gingered Carrots

SERVES 4

Of all the cooked vegetables I deplore, the worst is parsnips, closely followed by turnips, and then by carrots. All are insipid. I here make an exception. Gingered Carrots have authority. They may seem comparatively mild, but after one or two bites your mouth and throat will tell you you have not been eating creamed carrots or mashed potatoes.

3 cups carrot chunks	*1½ tablespoons brown*
3 tablespoons butter	*sugar*
2 tablespoons minced	*3 tablespoons ground*
scallion	*ginger*
3 tablespoons minced	*1 tablespoon freshly*
green bell peppers	*ground black pepper*

Cook carrots in a small amount of salted water until tender, about 10 minutes. Melt butter in another saucepan and lightly sauté minced scallion and peppers, then stir in brown sugar, ginger, and pepper. Drain carrots and add to the butter sauce. Stir until completely glazed and heated through.

Jamaican Beets

SERVES 4

The islands of the Caribbean produce many fiery dishes. While Jamaican Beets are not so fiery as some other recipes from the area, they have enough ginger to warrant inclusion here. The beets are so easy to prepare, you can, metaphorically speaking, do them with one hand, whether or not it knows what the other hand is doing. In a manner of speaking, they could be called the politician's vegetable.

2 teaspoons minced fresh	*1 one-pound can baby*
Jamaican ginger	*beets*
¼ cup sugar	*2 tablespoons butter*
2 teaspoons arrowroot	*1 tablespoon minced*
¼ cup cider vinegar	*parsley*

Place ginger, sugar, and arrowroot in a small bowl and mix thoroughly with a spoon. Slowly pour in the vinegar, stirring constantly to make a smooth mixture. Be sure that all the sugar has been absorbed and that no gritty granules have lumped together. Place the mixture in a heavy skillet large enough to hold the beets, and place over a medium heat, stirring with a wooden spoon until mixture reaches the consistency of rubber cement. Drain the beets and add to the skillet. Put in butter. Bring all slowly to a simmer and simmer, uncovered, for 10 minutes, being sure to coat the beets often and well. Serve very hot, garnished with parsley.

Pomodori Ripieni al' Inferno

SERVES 6

It is written that the serpent tempted Eve in the garden with an apple. But what kind of apple? Was it a Rambo, a McIntosh, a Grimes Golden, or, ironically, a Paradise? I don't think it was an apple at all but a tomato, which was known for centuries as a love apple and considered poisonous. Another controversy raged around the tomato: was it fruit or vegetable? Happily we now classify it as an edible vegetable.

As usually cooked, or eaten raw, the tomato is one of the mildest of vegetables. In this pseudo-Italian version, it acquires almost as much fire as the color of its skin would indicate. The tomatoes for my recipe should be ripe but firm. The best implement for removing the seeds and pulp is a grapefruit knife, but any small sharp knife will do. Do not skin the tomatoes as the skin reinforces the vegetable when it is under fire.

6 large tomatoes	*2 teaspoons Worcester-*
1 ten-ounce package	*shire sauce*
frozen chopped spinach	*2 tablespoons Tabasco*
2 garlic cloves	*2 tablespoons prepared*
8 slices prosciutto	*hot mustard*
½ teaspoon salt	*4 teaspoons grated*
1 teaspoon freshly ground	*parmesan cheese*
black pepper	

Preheat the oven to 400 degrees.

Cut off tops of tomatoes. Remove pulp and all seeds. Cook spinach according to package directions. Drain and let cool. Peel and mince garlic. Mince prosciutto. Rechop spinach and place in a bowl. Add prosciutto, salt, pepper, Worcestershire, Tabasco, and mustard. Mix thoroughly. Stuff tomatoes with mixture, and sprinkle each with a teaspoon of grated parmesan cheese. Place stuffed tomatoes in the preheated oven for about 15 minutes, until tomatoes and their contents are heated through. Remove to the grill and broil for 1 minute or until cheese is melted. Serve immediately.

Curried Green Tomatoes

SERVES 6

"She's a real, sad tomato, she's a busted valentine" is the refrain from a ballad popular some thirty-odd years ago. These green tomatoes differ markedly from the gal of the ditty. They are rich, not sad— they bring happiness; they have no connection with 14 February. The "tomato" of the night spots must have once been a "dish," the tomatoes of the recipe are still a dish: and as fiery as the lady of the ballad.

This recipe for curried green tomatoes, unlike a servant, can serve two masters: the vegetable chef and the salad chef. For either service you start by preparing the tomatoes the same way. When just cooked you may use them as a hot vegetable; when cool, as the principal ingredient of a salad. However you plan to use the tomatoes, you cook them this way.

1 medium onion	*¼ teaspoon ground cumin*
2 tablespoons butter	*¼ teaspoon ground*
4 medium green tomatoes	*cardamom*
2 teaspoons curry powder	*Salt*

Peel and chop the onion. Melt butter in a skillet and add onion. Cook over moderate heat, stirring occasionally to prevent onion's burning. While onion cooks, chop tomatoes coarsely into 1-inch cubes. Add curry powder to the skillet and continue to cook, stirring until curry powder begins to brown. Add tomato cubes, cumin, and cardamom. Maneuver the mixture until the tomato pieces are well coated with other ingredients, and are heated through. Taste. Add salt, if needed.

Bengali Brinjal

SERVES 4

Call it *melanzana, aubergine, barenjena,* or *brinjal,* it is still eggplant and good in any language. The Greeks have a word for it too: *melitsane.* Eggplant is sometimes a bland dish, but when Bengali cooks work with it, eggplant can become a fiery vegetable which will turn an otherwise vapid meal into one of élan and zest.

For this dish the eggplants should be bulbous, about 2 inches in diameter and weighing approximately 2 ounces each. If your greengrocer does not have them, try a Japanese greengrocer. The recipe takes about three hours to prepare.

8 small eggplants
Salt
1 medium onion
4 tablespoons rice
6 cherry tomatoes

2 teaspoons mint sauce
4 tablespoons vegetable oil
1 tablespoon curry powder
4 cups chicken stock

In preparing the eggplants be sure to maintain the integrity of the exterior, otherwise the dish will be soggy. Wash the vegetable in running water and dry carefully between towels. With a sharp knife cut off tops and reserve them. The next step requires extreme care. You need two implements—an apple corer with a blunt or squared off end, and a curved serrated grapefruit knife. Carefully center the corer in the middle of each eggplant and remove center of the pulp, slowly, so as not to puncture the bottom skin. Shift to the grapefruit knife and remove rest of pulp. (A thin layer of the pulp inside the skin will not damage the dish.) Place pulp in colander and sprinkle generously with salt. Cover pulp with aluminum foil and place a heavy weight on top of the foil—an iron or some canned goods— and let pulp drain for 30 minutes. Sprinkle additional salt around the insides of the hollow shells and let them stand upright for 2 hours. When pulp has drained, remove to a chopping board and mince. Place in a covered jar and refrigerate.

Preheat the oven to 375 degrees.

Peel and mince onion. Put in a bowl and add the rice. Skin and chop cherry tomatoes. Place in same bowl with onion, and add mint sauce. Stir well. Heat oil in a small saucepan or skillet and add curry powder. Stirring occasionally, fry until curry powder is dark brown. Simmer, still stirring, 3 minutes. Add cooked curry to the bowl along with the minced eggplant pulp. Blend contents of bowl thoroughly with a fork. Wash salt out of eggplant shells with cold running water. Drain. Fill shells with mixture in the bowl, tamping mixture down as you fill the shells. Replace reserved tops on the stuffed eggplants and fasten them in place with toothpicks. Arrange the stuffed shells, their tops upright, around the inside rim of a baking dish or casserole. Half fill the casserole with chicken stock and place in the preheated oven. Bake for 1 hour, or a little longer, occasionally basting with the hot chicken stock. Serve warm.

Zucchini Eureka!

SERVES 4

Finding a recipe which would justify the inclusion of zucchini in this cookbook was a problem. Research in all my cookbooks availed me nothing. I discussed the problem with several of my cookery consultants. One of them suggested a solution based on a meal she had had in Venice where the Italian vegetable was combined with the spices of the East. The recipe fitted the book. Like Archimedes, I shouted "eureka!" Hence the title.

1 cup freshly grated coconut	1 teaspoon turmeric
1 cup milk	1 teaspoon ground cumin
6 medium zucchini	1 teaspoon curry powder
1 large onion	1 teaspoon Tabasco
1 tablespoon butter	1 garlic clove
1½ tablespoons olive oil	Salt
	Fresh lime juice

Place grated coconut in a small bowl, add milk and let steep for at least 30 minutes, preferably 1 hour. While coconut steeps, wash zucchini and cut into ½-inch slices. Peel onion and slice thinly. Set aside. Melt butter and olive oil in a heavy skillet over low heat. Add to skillet the onion slices and cook until onion is translucent. Mix in the turmeric, cumin, curry powder, and Tabasco. When the mixture is hot through, cover skillet and remove from the stove.

Arrange a double layer of cheesecloth in a strainer over a bowl, and pour the coconut-milk combination into it. Twist the cheesecloth and force the liquid out into the bowl to make ⅔ cup coconut milk. Pour milk into the skillet. Half fill a large saucepan with water. Peel and halve garlic clove. Add to water along with about 1 tablespoon salt. Bring to a boil, add zucchini slices, and boil about 3 minutes. While zucchini boils return skillet to fire and stir its contents well to meld the curry mixture with the coconut milk. Drain zucchini and put into skillet over a low heat. Stir all together well, add a few drops of lime juice, and serve.

The Garbanzos of Granada

SERVES 4

Several years ago my wife and I were driving through southern Spain. As all good tourists should, we visited the Alhambra and the Generalife gardens in Granada. Some hours later, tired and hungry, we ate a typically late and typically Spanish lunch at a provincial inn. One of the vegetables was this splendid dish of fiery beans. We quitted the restaurant replete with food, the garbanzo recipe, but minus a considerable number of pesetas. The recipe, well worth the pesetas, is now yours.

Garbanzo is Spanish for chick-pea. In this country you seldom find them fresh. The dried version must either be soaked in water overnight, or may be prepared, as in the following recipe, in a matter of a couple of hours.

1½ cups dried garbanzo beans	*1¼ teaspoons turmeric*
1 teaspoon salt	*4 fresh mint leaves*
1 medium onion	*½ teaspoon dried hot chili peppers*
1 large tomato	*¾ cup condensed beef broth*
3 tablespoons butter	
½ teaspoon ground ginger	

Place beans and salt in a heavy saucepan. Cover with 3 cups of water and boil, covered, 3 minutes. Remove from heat and let stand an hour or two.

Peel and chop both onion and tomato. After the beans have soaked, replace saucepan on stove, bring contents to a boil, and simmer, covered, for at least 30 minutes. Drain beans, reserving stock. Return beans to saucepan. Melt butter in skillet, add onion and cook over moderate heat until the onion is translucent. Add tomato, ginger, turmeric, mint leaves, and chili peppers. Cook over medium heat for 10 minutes stirring the while to prevent burning. Pour over the beans. Mix well, add beef broth and enough of reserved bean stock to cover beans. Do not cover saucepan. Place over high heat and bring contents to boiling point; reduce to simmer. Simmer beans about 45 minutes or until most of the liquid has evaporated and the beans are well coated. Serve at once or keep hot in a double boiler until needed.

Hot Potatoes

SERVES 4

Hot potatoes are usually thought of as subjects or objects which you juggle to avoid burning yourself and pass on to someone else as quickly as possible. These hot potatoes, however, will not burn you, though they are both fiery and hot. Hence you will want to keep them for yourself. The recipe comes from a section of northeastern Maine where the inhabitants sometimes resort to fiery food to offset the bitter chill of their bleak winters.

8 medium new potatoes	*1 teaspoon Tabasco*
6 tablespoons butter	*1 teaspoon salt*
3 tablespoons prepared mustard	*2½ tablespoons minced chives*

Peel potatoes. Place them in a saucepan; immediately cover well with water and bring to a boil. Boil gently for 10 or 12 minutes. Add ½ cup of cold water, and boil another 5 minutes. The potatoes should now be done but firm. Drain. While the potatoes cook, melt butter in another saucepan. Add mustard, Tabasco, and salt. Mix ingredients well over a low heat. When the mixture is thoroughly hot, put in the boiled potatoes and coat them with the sauce.

When you are ready to serve, place potatoes and sauce in a serving bowl or tureen and garnish with a sprinkling of minced chives. Hot Potatoes make a moderately fiery vegetable which will add luster to an otherwise bland meal.

Candy Potatoes

SERVES 4

Never be misled by a title. If you doubt that axiom, this recipe exemplifies its worth. Your immediate reaction is to visualize sweet potatoes in treacle, perhaps with marshmallows as garnish. A ghastly thought! Misleadingly again, the candy in this instance is not a sweetmeat, but a city. It is also known as Kandy, capital of the central province of Ceylon. The Singhalese like fiery food and have developed recipes to suit their tastes, even one to fire up the potato, the blandest of vegetables.

8 medium new potatoes	¾ teaspoon cayenne
3 tablespoons butter	1 tablespoon milk
1 tablespoon dry	½ teaspoon salt
mustard	1½ tablespoons minced
1¼ teaspoons lemon juice	parsley

Scrub potatoes but do not peel. Half fill a 2-quart saucepan with water. Bring to a boil, put in potatoes, and boil about 15 minutes or until potatoes are done but still firm. Meanwhile make the sauce. Melt butter in a small saucepan, and add all other ingredients except the parsley. Mix all together well until you have a fairly thick mixture. Keep hot. When potatoes are done, drain, discarding water. Cut the potatoes into ½-inch slices and return them to the saucepan. Cover with the sauce. Using a wooden spoon, maneuver the potato slices and the mixture until each slice is well coated. Garnish with minced parsley and serve very hot. If they cannot be served immediately, the potatoes may be reheated over water in a double boiler, but do not steam them.

SALADS AND A SAUCE

F̲ew meals, in my opinion, are complete without a salad. This section is divided, therefore, into two parts: salads which are fiery in themselves, and one sauce. Because the latter is about the same consistency as French dressing, it could be used to make any salad as fiery as Stromboli in eruption. At least one other suitable use for it is mentioned. Your own skill and imagination may well suggest additional salads or other dishes where its fiery content will add to the taste.

Probably my hardest task in collecting recipes for this volume was to find fiery salads. I have been able to gather only a few. Those few are, however, eminently suitable. These salads, of course, should always be finally mixed with élan at table, and served with éclat.

Cerberus Salad

SERVES 4

Although they must have eaten during their tour of Hell, *The Divine Comedy* gives no indication of what Dante or Virgil were offered to stanch hunger. Whatever they ate, I suspect this salad was among the dishes. It is a subtle dish whose real effect is not immediately apparent. Part of the fire is provided by the dressing.

1 bunch watercress
1 bunch land cress
1 bunch parsley

2 large white radishes
½ cup strong Mustard
Dressing

Thoroughly wash the 3 bunches of greens. Then chop the leaves and stems and place them in a salad bowl. Scrape and cube the radishes. Sprinkle over the greens, cover the whole with the Mustard Dressing, toss well, and serve. The dressing provides the seasoning so no additional salt or pepper is needed in the salad itself.

Mustard Dressing

1 CUP

¼ cup red wine vinegar
1 tablespoon dry mustard
¾ cup olive oil
½ teaspoon salt

½ teaspoon freshly ground
black Java pepper
1 ice cube

Dissolve mustard in vinegar. Add other ingredients, except ice cube, and stir well. Just before using, add ice cube and stir until dressing begins to emulsify. Discard ice cube, and immediately pour dressing over salad.

Salade Anvers

SERVES 4

The origin of this Belgian recipe is unknown. My manner of getting it indicates that it was handed down from mother to daughter and never committed to paper.

The sprouts are essential and add much to both the appearance and crispness of the dish. They must be fresh, but if you wish to compose the salad when fresh sprouts are unavailable you may substitute half a cup of coarsely chopped green bell peppers with all seeds and membrane removed. The salad will be different but good.

Salade Anvers is fiery of itself, but if you use Mustard Dressing with it, you will have a three-alarm blaze. My wife, whose taste is highly discriminating, says, "it punishes the palate." I rather think it titillates the tongue. Whichever it does, serve it only with bland dishes.

3 large heads Belgian	*6 fresh Brussels sprouts*
* endive*	*8 cherry tomatoes*
4 long green chili peppers	

Cut off and discard bottoms of endive and slice the heads into rounds about ¾-inch long. Separate leaves and place in a salad bowl. Remove both ends of the chili peppers and slice peppers thinly, about ⅛ inch. Do not remove seeds. Sprinkle chili peppers over endive. Cut off bottoms of the sprouts and remove outer leaves. Cut sprouts into quarters. Place in bowl. Skin and halve tomatoes. Place them in a separate bowl. Just before serving the salad, add the tomatoes, and then any dressing you like as long as it is not mayonnaise-based.

Indonesian Cucumber Salad

SERVES 6

Technically this dish is not a salad. Perhaps it could be called a relish. Name it as you please, it is a fine accompaniment to curry. I had the recipe from a Dutch friend who lived for many years in Sumatra. He told me that this dish was a special favorite as a side dish with rijsttafel. The salad need not be reserved for curries or rijsttafel. It makes a good and reasonably fiery side dish at any time you require a relish. One added merit: it will keep, under refrigeration, for at least a week.

3 large cucumbers	*1 teaspoon ground*
2½ tablespoons salt	* ginger*
2 scallions	*1½ teaspoons turmeric*
3 garlic cloves	*1 teaspoon sugar*
1 tablespoon vegetable	*½ cup red wine vinegar*
* oil*	

Peel and halve cucumbers. Then quarter each half lengthwise. Remove and discard seeds. Cut cucumbers into ½-inch chunks. Place in a bowl and sprinkle with 2 tablespoons salt. Stir well and refrigerate for at least 1½ hours.

 Mince scallions and garlic. Heat oil in a skillet. Add scallions, garlic, and ginger and simmer, stirring occasionally. Add turmeric, remaining salt, and sugar. Stir. Add vinegar and 2 tablespoons water. Mix well once more, cover, and simmer contents of skillet for 10 minutes. While scallions, garlic, and ginger are cooking, remove cucumbers from refrigerator, and wash them well in cold water until salt has been removed. Drain and dry cucumber chunks between towels. Place the chunks back in the bowl. When contents of skillet have simmered the requisite 10 minutes, stir well, and pour, hot, over the cucumbers. Coat the chunks well and return to refrigerator until needed.

The chunks will be mustard colored. They should be brought to the table in a large glass salad bowl, or served in individual dishes or plates. In either case the cucumbers should rest gently on a few leaves of lettuce—preferably Bibb.

Cucumber Cooler

SERVES 4 TO 6

This salad is really a fire extinguisher rather than a fiery dish. You can make it fiery, if you like, by substituting cayenne for freshly ground black pepper. It is intended to accompany a curry but can well be used with any number of other fiery dishes, and some not so fiery.

I have been eating curries all my adult life and one problem has been to find a salad which could satisfactorily be served with or after curry. This salad, call it relish if you will, is perfect with curry.

16 ounces yogurt	*4 sprigs mint*
1 tablespoon white	*1 teaspoon dried dill weed*
vinegar	*Freshly ground black*
2 large cucumbers	*pepper*
Salt	

Place yogurt in a bowl and stir in vinegar to make a smooth mixture. Place bowl in refrigerator. Score cucumbers lengthwise with a fork, and cut into ¼-inch slices. Sprinkle cucumbers well with salt and set aside for 30 minutes. Mince mint. Place cucumber slices in a strainer and run water over them to remove salt. Drain and dry on paper towels. Return to bowl, and stir in mint and dill. Mix well into bowl of yogurt. Return mixture to refrigerator for 2 hours, but no longer. Just before serving mix ingredients again and place in a glass salad bowl. Sprinkle liberally with freshly ground pepper and additional dill and mint for garnish. Serve with or after curry as salad or relish. Delicious!

Der Drei-Rettige Salat
(Three-Radish Salad)

SERVES 6

This salad comes straight from a special, but short-lived Hell, established annually as a kind of one-night stand on Walpurgis Night in the Harz Mountains. There, the eve of May Day is celebrated by a gathering of covens. Members carry out well-prescribed rites in one of which a black goat has his throat slit. In my search for the book's dishes I was naturally interested in what food was proffered at these sabbats.

A friend, recently returned from Germany, spent thirteen years strolling, climbing, and crawling among the crags, crevasses, and tors of the Harz country searching for data on the regional eating habits, and particularly, on my account, to learn what he could about Walpurgis Night foods. Among other recipes, he brought back this salad. It is a dish made by the cooks of the covens, and as much of a natural for this book as a familiar is to a witch. The "three-radish salad" is intrinsically fiery, as you would expect from its origin, and need depend on no dressing to inflame it.

1 large bunch watercress	*4 tablespoons red wine*
1 black radish	*vinegar*
6 white radishes	*¾ cup olive oil*
24 red radishes	*¼ teaspoon salt*

Wash watercress thoroughly. Cut off and discard thick stems and chop remaining cress coarsely. Place in bottom of a salad bowl. Peel the outer skin of the black radish; cut the radish into ½-inch dice. Distribute evenly over watercress. Scrape white radishes and cut into small rounds. Toss indiscriminately over black radishes. Wash red radishes, remove stems and bottoms and cut into ¼-inch slices. Sprinkle over other contents of bowl. Place bowl in refrigerator. Mix vinegar, oil, and salt in a small bowl and set aside. Do not refrigerate. When you are ready to serve the salad, remove radish bowl from refrigerator. Mix dressing thoroughly again and pour over salad. Fold the dressing in with a wooden salad spoon and fork, and serve.

Because the radishes, especially the black and white ones, are indeed fiery you may wish to have a selection of unsalted crackers, or a tray of party pumpernickel available.

A Sallet of Onions

SERVES 6

Cave alium cepam! In the language of Lucretius the naturalist, you are warned. Eat not of this dish or serve it if you or your guests are planning to join others in social diversions after the meal. Avoid a dance at the country club, for example. Do not even sit at table with the salad if you have arranged for a later and promising tête-à-tête. The salad is what Dr. Johnson might have described to Mrs. Thrale as a "stinking, fiery dish." Being forthright and honest, the good lexicographer must have added that the sallet had appeal . . . for those who like onions.

1 large head Bibb lettuce	*1 cup ¼-inch slices of*
1 medium Italian onion	*leeks*
1 medium Spanish onion	*¾ cup chopped shallots*
1 medium Bermuda onion	*6 garlic cloves*
1 large sweet white onion	*2 Seville oranges*
½ cup ¼-inch slices of	*⅓ cup French dressing*
scallions, including some	
green tops	

Remove leaves from core of lettuce, and wash each leaf separately to remove all grit. Wrap lettuce in a dish towel and place in refrigerator to keep crisp. Peel Italian onion, slice very thinly and cut slices in half to make 1 cup. Repeat the process with the Spanish and Bermuda onions to yield 1 cup each. Peel the white onion, and slice very thinly. Without breaking the onions up too much, place them in a large bowl. Add the scallions, leeks, and shallots. Peel garlic cloves and mince or put through a press and add to bowl. Stir contents of bowl gently to mix all ingredients well. Set aside. Peel the oranges and slice them very thinly.

Arrange the lettuce leaves in the bottom of a salad bowl. Spread the contents of the onion bowl on top of the lettuce, and make a simple design of the orange slices atop the onions. Before actually serving the salad, pass the bowl around the table so that all may admire it. Place 2 or 3 orange slices on each of 6 salad plates. Pour the dressing over the salad, mix thoroughly, and distribute on top of the orange slices.

Een Sla van Nederlands Oost Indië
(A Dutch East Indies Slaw)

SERVES 6

Here is a delectable fiery salad from the Dutch East Indies. If you made it according to the original recipe only a starving man or one with an iron tongue, an asbestos palate, and a stainless steel throat could ingest it with equanimity. I have, therefore, taken liberties with the dish in the matter of cracked red pepper. Even I and my tasting team of international gourmets were able to eat but two or three mouthfuls of the salad made according to my Dutch friend's directions.

¼ cup shelled almonds
¾ teaspoon dried red chili pepper, chopped
¾ tablespoon sugar
1 teaspoon anchovy paste
4 tablespoons lemon juice
⅓ head iceberg lettuce
½ medium Chinese cabbage

½ medium cucumber
2 five-ounce cans thinly sliced bamboo shoots
6 scallions
2 large pimentos
2 cold hard-boiled eggs

Grind almonds and place in a bowl. Add chili pepper, sugar, anchovy paste, and lemon juice. Combine well and set aside.

Shred lettuce and Chinese cabbage and put in wooden or glass salad bowl. Remove skin from cucumber and, with a bean shredder, scrape thin strips of cucumber into the salad bowl. Drain bamboo shoots and put into same bowl. Cut scallions quite thinly, using most of the green tops, and set aside. Chop pimentos into ½-inch squares and put in bowl with the chopped scallions. Cut eggs into very thin slices. You are now ready to put the salad together. Add the anchovy paste mixture to the salad bowl. Stir ingredients together until they are well mixed. Sprinkle the scallions and pimento mixture over the salad and arrange the egg slices gracefully over the top to make an attractive garnish. Put salad bowl in refrigerator to chill for 20 minutes. Remove, and disturb salad violently with fork and spoon. Serve.

As I have said, this is an intense salad. Well-browned, buttered soft rolls would be a gladsome complement to it.

Four-Bowl Salad

SERVES 4 OR 8

Seldom do you find a dish that is both fiery and cold. More seldom do you find one which can be served either as a salad or as a main dish. Four-Bowl Salad can be a complete summer lunch for four or a salad course on a menu for eight. Preparing the salad is not so complex as the recipe makes it appear, but six hours are required for the salad to jell properly. The quantities given below make more than three pints. Discard the excess or freeze it for later use in toasted sandwiches. Do *not* fiddle with the amounts to make the recipe fit your mold.

8 hard-boiled eggs
1 large scallion
1 cup shelled cooked
  shrimp
½ large green bell pepper
6 red radishes
2½ cups chicken stock
1 tablespoon curry
  powder
2 tablespoons (enve-
  lopes) unflavored
  gelatin

1 teaspoon salt
4 tablespoons lemon
  juice
1 cup homemade
  mayonnaise
1 teaspoon cayenne
½ teaspoon Tabasco
1 large tomato
1 small head Bibb
  lettuce
6 sprigs watercress
Paprika

Split 4 eggs lengthwise and dice the other 4. Set aside, separating the large from the small. Chop scallion and halve shrimp. Place both in a bowl. Remove seeds and membranes from green pepper and dice. Chop radishes the same size. Add both to the bowl and set it aside. This is bowl I.

Place 2 cups of stock in a saucepan; add curry powder, gelatin, and salt. Warm stock, stirring the while, over a low flame until gelatin has dissolved. Divide contents of saucepan between bowls II and III. Stir remaining ½ cup stock and 3 tablespoons lemon juice into bowl II. With a damp cloth wipe inside of a 3-pint ring mold, but do not dry. From bowl II pour a thin layer of the mixture into mold and place in refrigerator until the stock is sticky but not stiff, about 4 minutes. Remove from refrigerator and put bowl III into refrigerator. Quickly arrange the split eggs, flat side down, around the mold on top of the gelatin. By now contents of bowl III should be syrupy. Spoon the contents over the eggs evenly and place the mold in refrigerator to set the stock.

Enter bowl IV, which should be larger than the others. Put in the chopped eggs and the contents of bowl I. Put in remaining lemon juice, the mayonnaise, cayenne, and Tabasco. Blend this mixture, gently, until the liquids are as one and the solids have been evenly distributed throughout. Chill lightly. When contents of mold are stiff—it should be when bowl IV has chilled 3 or 4 minutes—remove mold from refrigerator. Spoon contents of bowl IV into the mold, spreading evenly with a narrow, offset metal spatula and cover tightly with aluminum foil, plastic wrap, or wax paper. Keep the covering taut with a rubber band around the upper perimeter. Put mold in refrigerator and let stand relaxed and undisturbed for at least 4, preferably 6, hours before serving. (The salad will keep this way for at least 2 days.)

About an hour before serving, chill a circular platter larger than the mold, skin and cut the tomato into 8 wedges, wash the lettuce and separate enough leaves to decorate the edge of the platter. Chill leaves. When ready to present, and it is a presentation, arrange the lettuce leaves around the platter. Run a thin knife or spatula around the inside of the mold between the salad and the sides, including the inside ring. Turn mold upside down on the platter and apply a steaming, wet towel to the bottom, pressing hard to loosen the gelatin. Remove mold, and the salad, surrounded by lettuce, will be revealed in all its glory. Make a bed of watercress in the center, place the tomato wedges on top, and sprinkle the salad with paprika. Hot freshly made Melba toast goes well with the salad.

Shima Salad

SERVES 4

Normal green salads, good as they be, are not, to my taste, good companions for fish or seafood, especially the raw oyster. Precisely because it is so good a companion for that bland but succulent bivalve, I have named this salad after the city whence come the best Japanese oysters. I could have named it after Chincoteague, Lynnhaven, Shelter Island, or any number of other haunts of the oyster. But the recipe was given me by a remarkable Japanese girl, Atsuko Kitagawa, who, with three others, helped me consume something over a hundred raw oysters at a Sunday supper. She made the salad; I give the credit to her country. The salad was a perfect accompaniment. Its use need not be confined to an oyster menu. You will find many other occasions when its forceful flavor will enhance a meal.

1 finger fresh ginger 1¼-inches long by ¾-inch wide and ¾-inch thick	½ teaspoon sugar
	½ teaspoon salt
	¼ teaspoon freshly ground black pepper
1 green cabbage	¾ teaspoon monosodium glutamate
6 scallions	
½ tablespoon sesame oil	
½ tablespoon olive oil	1 teaspoon cracked red pepper
1 tablespoon fresh lemon juice	

Place ginger in a small bowl of lukewarm water and soak for 10 minutes. Remove outside leaves of cabbage and, with a sharp knife, shred cabbage about ¾-inch thick. Place in salad bowl. Cut scallions into ¼-inch slices using some of the green tops. The ginger should now be ready. Scrape off skin and grate the ginger with a fine grater into a small bowl. Add to the bowl the 2 oils, lemon juice, sugar, salt, pepper, monosodium glutamate, and cracked red pepper. Stir well to integrate all ingredients and pour over contents of salad bowl. Let salad marinate for about 15 minutes, and then toss thoroughly to coat all the cabbage and scallions. Serve at once, or place in refrigerator to keep cool if you want to present it after the main course rather than with it. The dressing may be used over many other salads to transform them from listless to fiery dishes.

Sauce

Penang Chili Sauce

YIELDS 1 CUP

Commercial chili sauce resembles this Malaysian version as Polly-anna resembled Cleopatra. The thick, red goo that oozes out of bottles is sweet and naïve. The thin, almost watery product of Penang has the fire of the woman who ruled an empire and a man who ruled another. Penang Chili Sauce adds fire to food which is already smoldering. My wife says this is another palate punisher, a pretty conceit. But I noted in Hong Kong, where we first met the sauce, that she used it extensively. A little of the sauce on almost any dish will make that dish more fiery. Putting it on already fiery food is akin to using gasoline to extinguish a blaze. The sauce is simple and will keep about two months if placed in a tightly capped sterilized bottle, and refrigerated. Do not use it with crab or oysters.

4 fingers fresh ginger, each about 1¼-inches long by ¾-inch wide and ¾-inch thick
4 large garlic cloves
2 dried red chili peppers

2 tablespoons chili powder
½ teaspoon sugar
½ teaspoon salt
1¾ cups cider vinegar

Remove outer skins from ginger and garlic and mince both. Mince chili peppers and discard about half the seeds. Place the above ingredients in a bowl. Add the chili powder, sugar, and salt. Mix well and place in a blender. Pour in the vinegar. Liquefy, running blender for about 30 seconds. Pour into a saucepan and, over very low heat, bring to a boil, stirring twice. When contents of saucepan come to a boil, remove from the heat and allow to cool. Strain through a chinoise, or a small strainer lined with cheesecloth. Using a wooden spoon, press mixture through the strainer until all liquid is expelled. Discard residue and bottle the liquid. You now have Penang chili sauce. You have also been told to treat it with the respect it deserves.

DESSERTS

Most of these desserts are fiery in the literal sense. Some of them are cold despite the flames surrounding them; Cherries Jubilee (page 171) is an example. The desserts fall under the book's title for two reasons. Flaming ones reflect the fires of Hell's upper circles; cold ones represent the two lower circles. In either case they are truly infernal.

Except for Queimado (page 175), fiery in both senses of the word, you can safely serve any of these desserts after any other dish in this book. I hope you enjoy the desserts: all are good and most make a pretty show with which to end a meal.

Crêpes Suzette

SERVES 4

"The fires of Hell rise 'round and sear us," comes, I think from a hymn. Perhaps it is an early martyrs' song. It has a special application to this and similar recipes. Hell's fires are stoked with brimstone which gives off a blue flame. So, too, does burning alcohol.

Crêpes Suzette recipes divide themselves into three parts: orange butter, the crêpes, and the sauce.

Orange Butter

½ pound (2 sticks) butter
2 tablespoons sugar
Grated peel of 1 lemon

Grated peel of 1 orange
Juice of ½ orange

Cream butter and sugar, and gradually add the rest of the ingredients, melding them until smooth. Cover and refrigerate.

Crêpes

YIELDS 12

6 tablespoons flour
2 tablespoons sugar
½ teaspoon salt

3 eggs
1 cup milk
Butter

Mix flour, sugar, and salt in a bowl. Beat eggs. Slowly add them, and the milk to the bowl and stir until smooth. Strain contents of bowl. Cover and refrigerate at least 1 hour before cooking the crêpes. Clarify butter and coat a 5- or 6-inch skillet. Pour about 1 tablespoon of batter into the skillet, tilt to cover the bottom of the pan, and cook over medium heat. Brown batter quickly on both sides, and with a cake turner remove the crêpe, which should be very thin. Place on a paper towel. Cover the crêpe with another paper towel and continue the process until you have used up the batter, buttering the pan from time to time as needed. When the crêpes are made, place them, separated by towels and wrapped with aluminum foil, in the refrigerator.

Sauce

Orange butter
2 tablespoons Cointreau
2 tablespoons Grand Marnier

6 tablespoons 151-proof Jamaica rum

Heat the crêpe pan over the burner of a chafing dish. Put in the orange butter and when it is melted add the crêpes, 1 or 2 at a time and heat them, turning now and then, until they are hot through. Fold them into quarters and move to one side of the pan. Continue until all are done. Now add the Cointreau and Grand Marnier, and the rum. As soon as the liqueurs and rum begin to vaporize, tilt pan until flame from the burner ignites the alcohol—giving off that beautiful blue brimstone flame. Stir the folded crêpes into the mixture and serve while the crêpes are still flaming.

Final flambéing at the table is good for the chef's ego. I commend it for that reason, even though the crêpes are not a new dessert.

Cherries Jubilee

SERVES 6

Like Crêpes Suzette, Cherries Jubilee give the chef an opportunity to show off his skill at the table and hence are praiseworthy. They are also a fine dessert and an extremely simple one. Furthermore, they flame like Hell itself.

1 24-ounce can Bing cherries	*½ cup 151-proof rum*
¼ cup cognac	*1 quart vanilla ice cream*

Drain the cherries and discard the juice. Place cherries in the blazer pan of a chafing dish. Pour the cognac and rum over them, cover, and bring slowly to a simmer. While the liquor is heating, serve the ice cream in 6 individual dishes. As soon as the liquor has started to simmer, uncover pan and set contents ablaze. Let the liquid burn for a few seconds while you spoon it over the cherries. Ladle a goodly quantity of the cherries and flaming liquor over the ice cream and serve at once. Devil's food cake is the obvious accompaniment to this dessert.

A Hellish Dessert Loaf

SERVES 6

In one respect this dessert is the epitome of Hell as described by Dante: it is composed of both fire and ice. Despite the ice, it smolders even though it does not flame.

While not so difficult as the Heraclean labors, finding shelled pistachio nuts is no simple task. You will probably have to settle for unshelled nuts in jars or plastic bags. The nuts will probably be salted. Do not wash them. Salt adds piquancy. You will require an oblong loaf pan or similar mold big enough to hold about five cups of liquid.

1 pint vanilla ice cream	1 tablespoon ground
⅓ cup shelled pistachio	cloves
nuts	1 cup heavy cream
2 tablespoons sugar	2 egg whites
1 tablespoon ground	¾–1 cup diced crystallized
cinnamon	ginger
1 tablespoon ground	1 tablespoon cognac
cardamom	6 maraschino cherries

Let ice cream soften enough to be spread. Sprinkle bottom of the loaf pan evenly with pistachio nuts. Cover them with the ice cream and smooth surface to an even depth. Place in freezer to solidify. Put the sugar, cinnamon, cardamom, and cloves in a bowl. Mix them thoroughly. Set aside.

Beat the cream until it is stiff but not buttery and put in refrigerator until the ice cream has solidified in the freezer. Beat egg whites until they peak. Remove whipped cream from refrigerator and gradually fold in the ginger, contents of the spice bowl, and the cognac. Do this gently, but see that the seasonings are completely integrated. Now add the beaten egg whites to the cream, and, again gently, mix to be sure spices are well distributed and the egg whites, cream, and cognac are evenly melded. Remove loaf pan from freezer. Fill with an even layer of the egg-cream-spice mixture. Cover pan tightly with wax paper and return to freezer. The pan should remain in the freezer a minimum of 3 hours, so you should start making the dessert about 4 hours before you plan to serve it.

Immediately before serving, remove pan from freezer and take off wax paper covering. With a long narrow spatula separate the dessert from the sides of the pan. Place the pan, upside down, on a serving plate and apply a very hot damp towel to the bottom. Tap bottom gently with the handle of the spatula. The dessert will drop out on the plate. Arrange 6 red maraschino cherries in a row along the top of the dessert. Cut dessert into even slices, as you would cut a loaf of bread, so that each diner has a cherry. The cherries add little to the flavor but much to the appearance. Fresh ladyfingers are good auxiliaries to this dessert.

Deep-Fried Ice Cream

SERVES 4

The last time I was in Kowloon, I drifted, rather unsteadily I fear, into a restaurant called Jimmy's Kitchen. Among other goodies on the menu, the dessert section listed "deep-fried ice cream." Obviously one had to try such a paradox. What I got was a brown ball a little bigger than a baseball. It was served with a sauceboat of flaming cognac, which the waiter ladled over the sphere. The ball was hot as Hell on the outside, hellishly cold in the middle, and brilliantly illuminated with a blue flame. What better *laissez-passer* could a dish have for entrance into this book? I asked the head waiter how the dish was made. He gave me the ingredients, one of which was sponge cake. We were interrupted before he could tell me how the cake was either cut, or baked so thin that it could be wrapped around an ice cream ball, as horsehide covers a baseball. This is a vital step. I left Hong Kong before I could continue my research. I could have written to resolve the problem, but being, as I am, lazy, and opposed to baking, I sought the help of friends. Only one came up with an acceptable answer. Her solution substituted commercial angel food cake for sponge cake, but was so like the original dish that the dessert now has a regular place among her menus. Combining what I learned in Jimmy's Kitchen with her solution, here is the recipe for Deep-Fried Ice Cream. You should allow two days for making it.

The ice cream may be vanilla, but pistachio, or butter pecan would be better.

1½ pints ice cream   *1 cup batter (below)*
2 loaves commercial
angel food cake

Allow ice cream to soften only enough to be malleable. Using your hands, mold ice cream into 4 balls and place them in the freezer. Next day slice cake crosswise ¼-inch thick. With scissors, cut the slices into 8 figure eights about 6-inches tall and 2½-inches wide at the shoulders. In the center the figures should be about 1½-inches wide: the Gibson Girl hourglass figure. The figures do not have to be exact. Remove ice cream balls from freezer and wrap each with a piece of cake. Use another slice of cake to cover the bare parts of the ball. Trim excess cake with scissors to make a smooth sphere. Return to freezer for another 24 hours at least.

About 2 hours or more before you are ready to deep fry the ice cream, make the batter:

⅜ cup flour	⅙ cup water
¼ teaspoon salt	¼ teaspoon vanilla extract
½ teaspoon baking powder	1 quart vegetable oil
1 egg	¾ cup cognac
⅓ cup milk	

Mix all ingredients except vegetable oil and cognac in a deep bowl. Place vegetable oil in a deep-fat fryer or saucepan and heat to 400 degrees if you have a deep-fry thermometer. If not, drop a cube of bread into the oil. If the cube browns in 30 seconds, the fat is ready.

Remove ice cream balls from freezer, cover them lightly with batter. Put in deep-fat fryer. When the balls are brown, remove and dry on paper towels. Meanwhile heat the cognac until it simmers. Place each ball in a cold dish. Ignite cognac and pour over ice cream balls. Serve immediately.

Simplicissimus

SERVES 4

Simplicissimus is a dessert for a harried housewife or the chafed chef. It can be organized in minutes and will be new to most of your guests. The ginger required comes in spheres, a little smaller than golf balls, and preserved in a very light syrup. Preserved Canton ginger is a ginger of different cut and is put up in a very heavy, sweet syrup. It is an unacceptable substitute for the lightly preserved ginger. You will likely find the ginger balls you need in specialty food shops or at oriental groceries.

Basically, the dessert is ginger and whipped or, as I once saw it on an American-Chinese restaurant menu, "punished" cream.

½ pint heavy cream	Syrup from ginger
12 balls preserved ginger	

Whip cream until very stiff. Refrigerate. Remove ginger from jar and with a sharp knife square off two opposite sides of each sphere so balls will stand upright on their bottoms and provide also a small plateau on top for the cream. Put 3 ginger balls in each of 4 dessert saucers. Pour 1 tablespoon of the syrup over each. Delicately arrange a small pyramid of whipped cream on each ginger plateau.

The best eating tools for this dessert are a sharp fruit knife, a fruit fork, and a teaspoon for eating—or should I say drinking—the syrup.

Queimado

SERVES 6

You might cavil at my including this medieval Spanish dish among desserts because it was originally served after the coffee which in turn followed the flans, cakes, and tarts. Frankly it is too good to leave out of any cookbook and far too appropriate to this specific one to be omitted. It is eaten with a small spoon from gold or silver saucers, if you have gold or silver saucers. China will serve. Queimado, which means a kind of burned drink, is literally fiery in every sense of the word. I have made some slight changes in the original recipe to render it more suitable for American usage. I suggest you serve it before or with the coffee.

According to a legend, queimado is a lovers' potion. The fire in and on it reflects the fire in their eyes, souls, and bodies. Mayhap 'tis true. Mayhap if after two bowls each they are not stone cold drunk on the floor, they pass the remainder of the night in an ethereal, if fuzzy, lovers' paradise. I can't vouch for the legend, but this is a most unusual dish both in appearance and taste.

Traditionally the dessert is prepared in large quantities for a score of dinner guests or for the entire tenantry of a grandee. It is usually made in a large copper cauldron with a long copper ladle for stirring and serving. The original recipe calls for *aguadiente*, a highly alcoholic brandy. This drink is almost impossible to find outside of Spain and for it I have substituted white 151-proof rum. I also substituted a heavy aluminum saucepan for the copper kettle and a silver ladle for the copper one. These changes should make it possible for you to prepare the dessert in your own kitchen without buying special utensils. The pears are my contribution to the dessert.

2 lemons

2 teaspoons sugar

4 whole cloves

1 four-inch cinnamon stick

⅔ cup light Barbados rum

⅔ cup cognac

6 tablespoons 151-proof Jamaica rum

3 ripe but firm pears

½ cup blanched almonds

Remove zest from both lemons and put it in a heavy saucepan. Add to saucepan the juice of the lemons. Add sugar, cloves, and cinnamon. Pour in the Barbados rum, the cognac, and the Jamaica rum. Allow contents of saucepan to steep for 20 minutes. Meanwhile, back at the cutting board, peel and core pears. Cut pears into bite-size pieces. About 15 minutes before you are ready to serve, place saucepan, covered, over low heat and bring contents gradually to a simmer. Divide pears and almonds among 6 very warm saucers. After contents of saucepan have simmered about 1 minute, ignite. The flames will rise so high you'll think you have opened Hell's front door. Let the flames die down a little, and ladle the blazing liquid over the pears and almonds. Serve while flames still rise from each dish.

Café Diable

SERVES 4

Café Diable—it is known also as café brulôt—deserves a place in this book, not only because of its name, but also because of the famous description of coffee as it should be: "Black as sin, strong as the Devil, and hot as Hell." Such coffee, especially when it is flamed as well, as is Café Diable, is potent enough to open the gates of Hell itself, were they ever closed. You can make Café Diable in any chafing dish.

1 large wide piece of lemon peel

1 large wide piece of orange peel

5 small sugar cubes

¼ teaspoon ground cloves

¼ teaspoon ground cinnamon

¼ teaspoon vanilla extract

1½ cups cognac

3 cups strong hot coffee

4 small twists of lemon peel

Place all ingredients except coffee, 1 sugar cube, and peel into the blazer pan of a chafing dish and bring to a simmer over low heat. Put a large gravy or other ladle into the mixture until the ladle is hot, a matter of a few seconds. Fill the ladle almost full with the mixture and add reserved sugar cube. Ignite the mixture in the ladle. When it is burning well, return contents of ladle to chafing dish. This will set the mixture afire. Add the hot coffee to the chafing dish and mix well. When the flame has subsided, pour the coffee into the small cups into which you have placed the twists of lemon peel. Serve at once.

Curried Cream Cheese Crêpes

SERVES 4

Blue blazes of flaming alcohol tend to monopolize hellfire desserts. Hence I am much pleased to conclude this section with a dish whose internal fire meets my high diabolical and epicurean stan-

The Hellfire Cookbook

dards. These curried crêpes are the more appropriate because their ingredients derive from all over the world. Among the places represented are the United States, India, Jamaica, France, and England. Hell's foundations may quiver at the shout of praise, but the laudations inspired by this dessert serve but to cement the crevices. By combining the cheese of Philadelphia, a curry paste made in England, and a chutney from Bengal, a chef contrived a filling for French crêpes and produced a fiery dessert of much merit which adds an extra fillip to the end of any meal. To heat his pancakes, and they should be served hot, the chef invented an admirable thin sauce. Like every true artist, he knew when to stop. He did not flame the brandy. The filling should be spread on the crêpes at the last minute, else they become soggy. The crêpes themselves are the same as those for Crêpes Suzette and like those crêpes, may be made some hours before they are to be used.

12 sweet crêpes (page 170)	*5 tablespoons Bengal chutney*
1 eight-ounce package cream cheese	*2 teaspoons curry paste*
2 lemons	*1½ tablespoons milk*
	¾ cup ginger brandy

Make crêpes and refrigerate until about 30 minutes before you plan to use them. Put the cheese in a bowl to soften. Grate the lemon peel and set aside. When cheese is soft, add chutney, curry paste, and milk. With a fork combine the ingredients into a smooth paste. Cover and keep in a cool dry place but do not refrigerate.

When you are ready to serve the dessert, spread the crêpes on one side with a substantial layer of the cheese mixture. Roll them into cylinders, spread side inside, and arrange them neatly in the blazer pan of a chafing dish. Heat slowly. Place the ginger brandy in a small pitcher and stir in the grated lemon peel. Pour half the brandy over the crêpes and continue to heat until the liquid begins to bubble. Place the crêpes on hot plates. Pour remaining brandy over them and serve immediately.

HELPMEETS

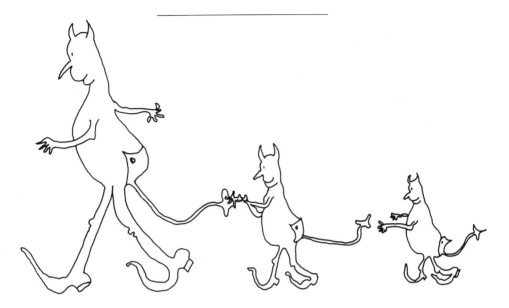

A helpmeet is one who helps you do something, an assistant. I use helpmeet in a slightly different sense: to help you meet emergencies which might arise in preparing the preceding recipes. In short, this section is a catchall which lists items not necessarily found in the average kitchen or larder but which you will need. I have divided the section into three parts.

The first is called "Fuel for the Flames," and includes spices and herbs frequently needed to make dishes fiery. Presumably you already have Tabasco and Worcestershire sauce, curry powder, as well as black and cayenne peppers. But have you, for example, cracked red and black peppers, or fenugreek, and spices required to compound curry powder? Have you little, hot red and green chili peppers?

The second part, "Fire Extinguishers," offers food suggestions intended to keep you and your guests from being orally and internally incinerated by too much or too many of the items in the first part. Party pumpernickel is one such item. It can be kept frozen for considerable time, but thaws quickly and is better than any liquid as an antidote to the fires started by some of the recipes.

The third part is a compilation of condiments and relishes you will need, especially with curries. Some fan the flames, others tend to reduce them. Mostly these are relishes and chutneys, and mostly they come in jars and will keep for many a moon. Recipes for the home manufacture of some of these comestibles can be found in a few general cookbooks, with one exception—Penang Chili Sauce (page 165). The items listed below are guides only and you may wish to add to them.

Fuel for the Flames

Allspice, ground
Cardamom pods, whole
Cardamom seeds, ground
Chili peppers, green
Chili peppers, dried red
Chili powder
Cinnamon, ground
Cinnamon sticks
Cloves, ground
Cloves, whole
Coriander seed, ground
Coriander seed, whole
Cumin seed, ground
Cumin seed, whole
Curry paste
Fenugreek seed
Garlic, fresh cloves
Garlic powder
Ginger, crystallized
Ginger, fresh

Ginger, ground
Ginger, preserved (not Canton)
Horseradish, powdered
Horseradish, prepared
Horseradish root
Mango juice
Mirin (Japanese wine)
Mustard, dry
Mustard, prepared, hot
Mustard seed, whole
Nutmeg, ground
Nutmeg, whole
Pepper, cracked black
Pepper, cracked red
Peppercorns, black
Peppercorns, white
Rum, 151-proof white Jamaica
Rum, Barbados light
Saffron, shredded
Turmeric, ground

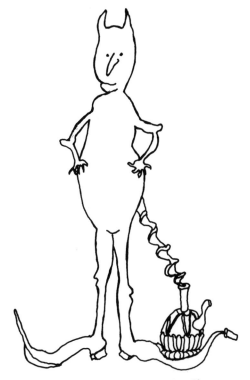

Fire Extinguishers

Ale
Beer
Wines; Sake
Bread: French, Italian, or Spanish
Melba toast
Pappadums
Pumpernickel, thickly sliced
Pumpernickel, thinly sliced party loaf
Sesame-seed crackers
Syrian bread
Tostados

NOTE: The ales, beers, and wines are palliatives only; they do not extinguish Hell's fire but momentarily relieve its stress. Sweet soft drinks, for example, do not cure thirst except briefly, then they increase it.

Condiments and Relishes

Almonds
Bombay duck
Coconut, fresh grated
Coconut, frozen grated
Codfish, dry flaked
  (substitute for Bombay duck)
Currants
Peanuts, roasted
Pineapple, unsweetened rings
Raisins

Chutney, green tomato
Chutney, hot Bengal
Chutney, hot fruit
Chutney, Major Grey's mango
Chutney, onion
Chutney, red tomato
Jelly, black currant
Jelly, red currant
Pickles, mustard
Relish, hot red pepper
Relish, hot tomato
Relish, mango
Relish, sweet pepper

Index